WHEN CRESCENT AND CROSS CONVERGE

WHEN CRESCENT AND CROSS CONVERGE

Lessons in Life, Love and Respect

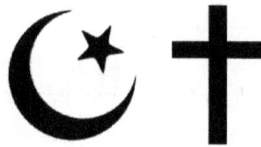

☪ ✝

IQBAL AND AMY ATCHA

When Crescent and Cross Converge: Lessons in Life, Love
    and Respect

by Iqbal and Amy Atcha

Artwork by Michael Telapary
    http://www.tewanka.com

Design, layout, and editing by Christopher Lake
    http://www.cmlstudios.com

ISBN–13: 978–0615613154

For information about special discounts on bulk purchases,
please contact us at:
    Converging Worlds
    630.965.6303
    http://www.convergingworlds.com

    Customized Caring
    630.306.4480
    http://www.customizedcaring.com

*This book is dedicated to the hundreds
of thousands of couples involved in an
interracial or interfaith relationship and
the people who know and love them.*

*This book is also dedicated to those
individuals who are genuinely interested
in learning how to connect with others
of different cultures and faiths.*

Contents

Acknowledgments

We would like to thank our parents,
Ismail and Zulekha Atcha,
and Tom and Judy Arcy,
for the love, guidance and experiences
you have given us over the years.

We would also like to thank our children,
Haroon, Kimberly and Hassanah,
for testing our strengths as parents and providing
loving memories that we will cherish forever.

Preface

Of the 7 billion people on planet Earth, approximately 32 percent are Christian, 22 percent are Muslim and 13 percent are Hindu. The remaining 33 percent are a combination of various faiths including Judaism, Buddhism and Taoism.

So why does this matter? Religion and race have become increasingly meaningful in our daily lives but they have become increasingly controversial as well. Whether it was the events of 9/11 or the election of Barack Obama, religion and race have become a powerful catalyst for love and unity *or* hatred and fear — depending on which side you stand.

Racism and bigotry exist in every corner of the world. People are still judged by the color of their skin, language, ethnicity, background, social status, lifestyle, and religious beliefs. No matter how nice a person may be and no matter how caring they are, certain people never see beyond a stereotype.

When others discover that Iqbal is an Indian/Pakistani Muslim and that Amy is a Polish/Irish Catholic, they often ask, "How does that work?" Many want to know how we "reconcile" the differences between our faiths and cultures. People fear the unknown — this includes other human beings as well.

After hearing that question over and over again, we decided to share our story. People were curious and wanted to learn how we not only overcame our fear but how we built a life based on our differences. They were interested to find out how we made things work.

So often when you hear the words "Crescent and Cross," you automatically think "tension" and "hostility." Nowadays, those terms are viewed as polar opposites and the collision of the two, especially in news reports, is comparable to mixing oil and water. Out of ignorance or anger, people say things that simply don't make sense but others are quick to believe.

We are all human beings. Every single one of us feels joy, suffers pain and bleeds red. Being human encompasses these emotions and so much more. Being human rises above the stereotypes and labels people give each other so freely but without basis.

In this book, we share with you our thoughts, our beliefs and ourselves. Most importantly, we share with you the lessons we have learned throughout our friendship and marriage. These lessons are of life, love and respect not only for each other, but for all people in this vast and magnificent world.

We wanted to set the record straight. We wanted to explain to everyone that what you see on TV or what you hear on the radio is *not* an accurate portrayal of day to day life. Instead, we show you that the opposite exists. We show you what happens "When Crescent and Cross Converge."

CHAPTER 1

Who Am I?

When people ask me "Where are you from?" I can't help but laugh. I've been asked this question so many times and I've gotten the same exact response that I think I've figured out what they're expecting. People want to hear a one minute story about my culture, some insights into my religious upbringing and a personal experience or two that can neatly define me. The problem is that I can't make it simple.

For starters, my name "Iqbal" is Pakistani, but my mom is from India, my dad is from Burma, I was born in New Jersey ("Joizee" for those of you from the shore) and I grew up in Chicago. So I laugh, because everyone I tell that to looks at me with that "deer in the headlights" look and then they want to know more. They want to hear the whole story so they can try and make sense of my life. Let me save you "that look" and I'll start from the beginning.

To know me, you have to know a little bit about my parents. Without them I wouldn't have even been a twinkle! Ismail and Zulekha met each other through some family matchmakers and dated for about two years. Back then, dating was called courtship and it was always with adult supervision, which my parents never forget to remind me. Anyway, they got married in 1964 but life for them wasn't the fairy tale they had imagined.

The Burmese military had overthrown the government and had taken over the country. This, plus the growing wave of Burmese nationalism (that's the nice way of saying racism and prejudice) made life pretty difficult for our family and friends. The Burmese were angry that "foreigners" were in their country, taking their jobs and sending their money back home. Now although my father was born in Burma and was a Burmese citizen, he wasn't really Burmese. Both of my grandparents had left India and moved to Rangoon (now called Yangon) and the natives called folks like that "Khway-Kullaw" or "dirty dog foreigners."

The breaking point came one morning when the Burmese military chained the doors to my grandfather's business. They seized control of every foreign owned store that day and my family put two and two together pretty quickly. They realized that they needed to find a way out of Burma before the threat of violence became a reality. Coincidentally, the Vietnam War was in full swing and that had created a shortage of doctors in the U.S. My dad, a medical doctor for the Burmese Navy, was eager to answer that call. So my parents packed their bags in 1969 and moved to the land of the free and home of the brave.

It wasn't just war that brought my parents to America. Like most immigrants, my parents came here looking for a better life. My dad worked two jobs at the hospital and my mom worked as a secretary until I was born in 1971. Even with a new baby, my parents managed to scrimp and save every penny they could until they had saved enough to bring my grandparents and older brother over from Burma. We were one big happy family living in one tiny little house, but it was home.

It's what I'd call a very traditional Indian-Pakistani home too! Dad went to work early every morning and came home late every night. You could smell the distinct aroma of cumin and curry whenever you walked in the door and our record player never stopped spinning Indian albums. While the adults cooked and cleaned, my brother's job, and mine (if you could call it that) was to study, study, study! It was the standard way of life in every Indo-Pak house, at least that's what my friends and I believed.

I didn't think living with my grandparents was weird, even though my friends did. In fact, it was pretty amazing and there were a lot of advantages to it too. Besides the basics like having four adults to play with and help me with my homework, I always got a double helping of dessert. If Mom *and* Dad said no, I'd go ask my grandparents to which of course they'd always say yes! It was better than pitting Mom against Dad and it always had better results!

All fun aside, it was my grandfather (who my brother and I called Nana) that taught me my faith and my outlook on life. Nana was my "godfather" and he taught me how to read the Quran in Arabic and how to pray. He was the one who taught me that *all* the prophets, from Adam to Muhammad (peace be upon them), were hand-picked by God and they should all be respected regardless. It was Nana who instilled in me a connection between all human beings. His compassion and conviction for helping people, regardless of faith, color, race or social status, left a lasting impression on me. I have no doubt that it's because of him I am who I am today.

My grandmother (Nani) focused less on faith and more on culture. Every Sunday night, my brother and I would sit by her feet while she'd massage coconut oil into our hair to make it all shiny and healthy. She'd tell us stories about what life was like growing up in the late 1800s as the youngest daughter in a very rich family. It was strange and exciting to hear about the servants she had, what society and religion were like at the time and what life in rural India meant. My favorite story was about her uncle who spent decades learning how to control a spirit (what we call jinn) and how harnessing that power destroyed his family and drove him insane. There were so many stories and a lot of coconut oil bottles too! But it was those nights that connected me to her, my past and the legends that Nani shared with us.

Just as much as my family helped shape me, the community I lived in did as well. I grew up on the north side of Chicago, a virtual melting pot of global cultures and faiths. We lived right in the middle of what was called "Little Israel," a one square mile of Jewish homes and businesses. Despite growing tensions in the Middle East and the fact that we were one of only two Muslim families living in Little Israel, we had a very peaceful existence with our neighbors.

But there wasn't just a Little Israel either. Surrounding it was a Little India, a Little Russia and a Little Korea. There were no welcome signs or border crossings but you could tell you were in a different neighborhood by its sights, smells and sounds. Walking to and from school every day, I could tell how far I still had to go by the smell of fresh lox and bagels, masala dosa or spicy kimchi. On Saturdays, I would play outside and watch Orthodox Jews, dressed in black with long beards and curls on the side of their heads, walk side by side with "Progressive" Jews (clean shaven men with yarmulkes) towards one of the many synagogues in the neighborhood.

When my parents took me shopping in Little India, I'd hear the women admire the brightly colored saris and the men argue (what my family calls negotiations) over the price. What seemed strange to me then and even now is how everyone stayed in their own neighborhood. Indians didn't go into Avi's bakery for challah bread and Jews never bought curry or turmeric from Dipak's grocery store. People consciously avoided interacting with their neighbors and it kept me wondering why.

School was a different microcosm of fun. No one really notices you're different when you're in the third grade, but things definitely change once you start junior high. Half of the kids in my class were from India, Korea and Eastern Europe. But just like the neighborhoods we lived in, we didn't cross borders and make friends easily. To make matters worse, our "American" classmates didn't want to hang out with us either. Most of them thought all of us were "uncool." Maybe it was because we weren't extroverts or because some of us spoke with an accent. We didn't act, think or worry about being cool because our main focus was getting good grades. That was reason enough for them to pick on us and beat us up.

I can't prove it, but I'm pretty sure they singled me out more than others. Call it the price for being "head of the class" or "teacher's pet" but getting shoved into the girls' line, being stabbed in the leg with a pencil and getting attacked by a gang of four or five guys in an empty classroom wasn't the typical stuff my friends talked about. I never told a teacher or my parents because I was scared of somebody retaliating, but I definitely wanted it to stop.

I remember begging my dad every week for years to let me take Karate or Kung Fu. I figured if I could at least defend myself, I'd be OK. But every week, my dad would remind me that my studies should be my number one focus. I felt trapped an awful lot but I never gave up hope that one day, I would protect myself and my friends just like Bruce Lee and Jackie Chan.

Ironically, it was my grades that eventually saved me. Being in the top 10 percent of my class, I was enrolled in a college prep school: Lane Tech. The rest of the class had to enroll at the local high school: Mather. It was the taste of freedom I had dreamed of for years and with this fresh start, I was determined to reinvent myself. By the time I was a sophomore, I had transformed from a "brown brainiac" into a cigarette smoking, long-haired metal-head. The "tough-guy" image protected me and my friends from the "jocks" and "stoners" but it didn't change my beliefs. I was comfortable with who I was and with what I believed. I still got good grades and I still believed what my Nana had taught me.

In my junior and senior year, I joined India Club and got to experience the biggest multi-cultural event I've seen to this day. Lane Tech's International Days were a two-day festival where clubs of different ethnicities performed native dances and served traditional foods. It was this event that made me realize what makes us all brothers and sisters; everyone loves good food and we all love to dance! I may not be a big fan of Korean kimchi but give me some Thai chicken satay, Italian meatballs and a Polish punchki and I'm good to go! High school was a *fantastic* experience and it taught me how to respectfully interact with people from different backgrounds and beliefs. Little did I know that college life would put these skills to the test.

My father picked Loyola University as the college I would attend. That may come as a shock to some of you but it wasn't for me. I wasn't thrilled with not being able to live in the dorms, experiment with new things and live my life away from the watchful eye of my parents. But the reality of the situation was two-fold: 1) in my culture, respect for your parents includes placing their desires over your own, and 2) he was paying for the whole thing. So why did my dad pick a Jesuit-Catholic university to send his Muslim son to? His reasons were simple: it was a prestigious university that was close to home. Who was I to argue?

Loyola was nothing like what I had seen in the movies. There was no late-night partying, no hazing and no girls looking for a good time. Come to think of it, that's probably why my dad picked it too! Fifty percent of the students were Caucasian and Christian (much like junior high) but the environment was totally different. Everyone was very open to making friends with people of different nationalities, cultures and faiths. Best of all, there were no borders, physical or imaginary. In fact, the Muslim Student Association, Hillel (the organization of Jewish students and faculty) and other cultural groups collaborated several times a year to sponsor an event or to promote an idea on campus.

Loyola was different from other colleges in a lot of ways. The biggest difference, though, was that all students had to take two semesters of Christian theology. It was part of the curriculum and classes were taught by Jesuit priests. I wasn't thrilled with the idea at first but after a few weeks, I fell in love with it! I learned about the origins and principles of Christianity and how they were being applied to problems both big and small around the world. What fascinated me the most was how similar the Old Testament and the Quran were. Both holy books spoke on the same issues, shared the same message and emphasized the importance of expressing love and kindness to our fellow human beings. One priest in particular, Father Gene Szarek, was like no other. His outgoing personality, knowledge of Islam and willingness to engage in religious discussions with me left an indelible and positive mark on my life.

While we all have an idea of how things should go, life doesn't always work that way. I had planned on pursuing medical school after graduating from Loyola but instead, I got married my junior year of college and became a father to a bouncy baby boy. Undeterred, I continued to take classes and graduated with a Bachelor's degree in Biology. Three years later, I became the father to a cherub faced baby girl. It was rough, but I continued to live with my parents while I worked full-time and applied to graduate school. I was finally accepted into the pharmacy program at Midwestern University (with my father's blessings) and began a new chapter in my life.

My class at MWU consisted of Caucasians, Asians, Africans, Indians and a smattering of "others" but we all treated each other like family. Since home was an hour and a half away, it was common for me to sleep in a friend's dorm room the night before an exam. Mayur, a practicing Hindu, was one of those friends who treated me more like a brother. Not only did I have a "bed" in his tiny dorm room but he'd cook dinner for me too so I wouldn't starve. After graduation, many of us went our separate ways but Mayur and I actually grew closer. We started a business together, celebrated birthdays and helped each other through hard times, including my divorce. It was living proof that friendship is not defined by labels or dogma but by spirit.

Since graduating in 1999, I've worked with pharmacists and patients of all faiths and cultures. I am blessed to have served people in the poorest communities of Chicago alongside African Americans, Arabs, Indians and Latinos. Most of my friends and family openly expressed their concerns about my safety working in "such a dangerous area," but their loss was my gain. Even in those blighted communities, there was a level of respect, loyalty and honor not many understand.

The pharmacy I worked at had been highlighted on WGN-TV as the "murder capital of Chicago." It was common knowledge not to be out on the streets after dark, but the gang-bangers knew that anyone with a white jacket (namely doctors, pharmacists and nurses) were there to help. They needed our help and they wanted it too. Not so much for themselves but for their "grammas," "baby mamas" and their kids. It wasn't uncommon for me or my staff to get a personal escort from the doorway to the car some evenings. It was a glaring reminder that all people, black or white, rich or poor, protect the ones they care for and show kindness because they can.

So who am I? After 40 years, I still struggle to answer that in 60 seconds or less. There's no simple definition. I'm a Muslim who loves taking care of people in need. I'm a pharmacist, an author, a speaker, a business owner. I'm a son, husband, father and friend. I'm a product of the love, trust and kindness others have shown me. In short, I am human.

Who Am I?

✝

Who am I? Well that's a good question. In truth, I suppose I am several people all wrapped into one. My husband used to tease me and say, "of course you are, you're a Gemini!" But I think I'm actually more than just the "two twins." I really am several people — a mother, a daughter, a wife, a friend, an employee, a businesswoman, a speaker, and an author. I am also half Polish, half Irish, and 100 percent Catholic.

To make a long story short, I was born in Michigan and raised with my three brothers in a typical Midwestern fashion. My parents, Tom and Judy, were both teachers. We lived in a modest home, had the old brown family station wagon and at various time had either a cat or a dog. I was a special child and knew it right away — you see, I was the only girl. In some respects, I had all the privileges of an only child — my own room, new clothes (never any hand-me-downs) and lots of dolls and stuffed animals. But I had it even better because I also had three brothers! Two of them, Jeff and Dan, were older, and Matt (the baby of the family) was a year and a half younger.

You might have thought my parents were crazy to have four kids in only five years, but now that I look back on it, it was actually very nice. We all played together and our activities were even similar. Of course, there were the usual differences — I was in Girl Scouts, took ballet and baton lessons and played the flute — but all of us kids also swam. In fact, I started swimming competitively by the time I was seven years old. I'll never forget that first, long — seemingly never ending — race across the pool, with me wearing my bright blue racing suit with the red stripe down the side and my lovely white swim cap (I had really long hair then). I was so proud of myself for finishing — and I got a ribbon! I was ecstatic!

Swimming carried over into our lives when we left Michigan and moved to Ames, Iowa. I was in the fourth grade then and Ames was where I really "grew up." Ames was a smaller-sized city with a university (Iowa State) on the edge of town. We only had one high school — Ames High — and only two movie theaters. Even by today's standards, this alone meant it was a small town.

The friends I made in fourth grade continued to be my friends until I graduated from high school and some even beyond. Mostly I just hung out with the "swimmers," going to practice before and after school almost every day. The weekends were spent in a typical Midwestern style as well — going to swim meets, working at the pool and at a gift shop, going to the movies and out for pizza and studying, if need be. Nothing too crazy.

School was the place to hang out with friends and live out the drama in our teenage lives. Having brothers so close to my age was both a blessing and curse. By the time I got to high school, the teachers already knew my name (there was only one Arcy family in town) and many knew me from swimming as well. The down side was that I never actually had a date. Having two protective, physically intimidating athletes as older brothers doesn't make you the girl everyone dreams of dating — or they might, but they never acted on it. In fact, I never even went to prom. I did go to Winter Formal though — that was a "girl-ask-boy" dance. But I'll say, even then it was tough to get a date. When I asked one boy, "Do you want to go to the dance with me?" he replied, "I can't do that! That would be like dating my sister!" Thus my love life was rather limited.

My brothers and I were pretty close, having many of the same friends — mostly all from other swimming families. We'd ride to school every day in the same car, see each other in the hall and acknowledge each other only if we had to. One day during my junior year stands out though — a day that I'll never forget. It was a cold, rainy fall day and as usual we were running late for school. The car wouldn't start and we had to take the motorcycle. Dan got the helmet since he was driving (we only had one) and I got to hang on to the back of the bike with water dripping off my face. Needless to say, neither Dan nor I were in a particularly good mood by the time we made it into the school parking lot. We jumped off the bike, me rushing in one direction and Dan in another, both of us trying to get to our lockers and then to class before the bell rang. I didn't see Dan again until a couple hours later, in between classes. When we passed each other in the hall, we both stopped dead in our tracks and stared in disbelief.... We were dressed *exactly* alike! We both had on the same gray sweater, jeans and our hiking boots! Other than the obvious fact that I was a girl and had my hair in a pony tail — we looked identical! How embarrassing! When our friends saw this, they burst out in uncontrollable laughter.

Nevertheless, I survived the social life in school without too much trouble. My classwork was typical of most college prep programs. I took physics, chemistry, algebra, English and Spanish along with a few other electives mixed in. I never gave college a second thought. Of course I was going, just like all my friends and essentially my whole graduating class. I was so sure that I wanted to go to Iowa State that I didn't even apply anywhere else.

Now let me back up just a bit to the summer before my senior year. As with my parents, my grandparents were also big proponents of learning, both from the classroom teaching view as well as from practical real life experiences. As an early graduation present, my grandparents sent each one of us kids on a three week trip through Europe, during the summer before our senior year in high school. It was their gift to us to be able to share the joys and mysteries of the world and through our stories, be able to live it themselves.

Although I didn't realize it at the time, I eventually came to appreciate my international trip. It was my chance to see that there was, in fact, a whole wide world outside the four corners of Iowa and that nothing (and no one) could hold me back from my pursuits. I'll admit however, that I didn't quite absorb the full effect of this at the time since I was only 16 years old.

That summer, I traveled through Europe and the Mediterranean with a group of high school kids from my surrounding area. We, in turn, joined up with a couple of other high school groups from the U.S. In London, Paris, Rome and Athens, I was exposed to many different cultures and experiences. The sights, the sounds, the smells in each city were all more amazing than the last! Then, with my eyes opening a little wider every day, I had the opportunity to visit Egypt and Tunisia, where I rode a camel and visited a mosque. To this day, I can recall in great detail the beauty of one particular mosque in Tunis — it was like an elegant shining mirage in the desert! I had never seen anything like it before, nor like it since. The intricate detail of the carvings and the white tile were breathtaking. The interior of the building was one enormous room, like a large courtyard. But above all, the most amazing part of that oasis in the sand was the calm and peace of the surrounding environment. It almost made time stand still; I could have stayed there for hours.

From a cultural perspective, taking that trip was when I truly realized that there were other people in the world, some very different from me. You see, while growing up in Ames had its advantages (we never needed to lock our doors and any neighbor would be glad to help you out), we also never got to experience the diversity that the world brings. Sure, we had a couple of African-American families in town and a few Asians as well. But for the most part, all of Ames (not including the university) was Caucasian and Christian.

I did mention that I am Catholic, right? I was baptized shortly after I was born and took my first communion during second grade while living in Michigan. After moving to Iowa, I was "confirmed" in our Catholic church with a group of other ninth-graders that I went to school with. In my house, going to church every weekend was also required (Mom's rule) at least until we graduated from high school. So on most Saturday evenings for 4:45 PM mass, the family would load into the car and off we went. Like I said, this was the rule, even in high school.

I also attended catechism (or CCD as we called it then) in the church basement every Wednesday evening. I'll admit I skipped a time or two, opting to go out for a burger instead. But for the most part, I went to the church along with about 30 or 40 other kids. I enjoyed going too — sitting in groups and being led by a counselor, we discussed the Catholic perspective to those "teenage" questions such as pre-marital sex, abortion, and drugs. My beliefs fell right in line with the rest of my friends — in today's words, we would probably be viewed as "pro-choice" even though the official Catholic position was then (and still is) "pro-life." Being the teenagers that we were at the time, we knew everything and felt we had the right to make our own decisions, especially when it came to these sensitive and very grown up issues.

But back to the story … basically, it was just a "given" that I went to mass with the family every weekend — no questions, no fights — just acceptance. Since most of my friends and other high school kids were there too, it was just part of everyday life in Ames, Iowa. I even served as an altar girl at some of the masses — rather progressive for the Midwest!

In addition to going to church, the religious perspective in our home was Catholic as well. Not realizing it at the time, this was especially helpful to me when I was going through those teenage years. At about this time, I found and fell in love with the poem "Footprints in the Sand," by Mary Stevenson, which I still read on occasion. I've included it at the end of the book if you want to read it yourself. The gist of the poem is that no matter what, God (Jesus) is with you and in those tough times, He is actually carrying you through — you're never alone. This is a very strong belief that I still have — and at times need to remind myself even to this day.

When I finished high school and went on to college, things stayed pretty much the same from the religious perspective — although I didn't seem to make it to church quite as regularly. The majority of my friends and acquaintances were other Christians and religion itself was rarely discussed. I just accepted that basically everyone was a Christian of some denomination.

Then, during my sophomore year at ISU, I took a class on World Religions. I found it fascinating! Although it was only for the semester, it got me thinking about the world again, the different cultures and the ways that people believed in "that Higher Being." I still remember sitting in the library doing research on Buddhism, Taoism and Hinduism, not realizing how the hours were flying by. That was my start to learning and sharing the wide world that we live in — from the religious perspective.

I enjoyed that class so much so that I signed up for a few other religion classes. I even thought that perhaps I'd get a minor in Theology. Unfortunately, as all good things do, this new found passion waned when I took a class on the Bible — a literal interpretation. A few days into the class, I realized that I was having a hard time grasping the concepts in the class. The discussions made no sense! That's when it dawned on me — we were discussing the Bible from a scientific and literal approach! When the realization hit me, I knew I had to drop the class. This way of thinking conflicted greatly with how I had been raised — to believe, not to question the scientific possibility of faith and miracles, etc. My mind just could not adjust (even if only for the semester) that the events of the Bible were not physically possible. I was taught and wanted to believe what was written, even if it was figurative prose.

I still find different religions fascinating. I have a book at home entitled "Religions of the World" that gives a description of about 15 different faiths. It's not unusual for me to pick up that book, especially on a mellow weekday evening and read a chapter wondering, "do I know anyone that practices this?" and "how does it differ from Catholicism?"

In 2000 and 2001, I again had the opportunity to travel abroad and experience a new culture — this time in Poland. Although I was there for work (the U.S. Department of Labor was helping the Polish government establish a private pension regulatory system), I was able to wander the back streets of Warsaw experiencing the culture, as well as partake in some of the traditional sightseeing and tourist activities. Oddly enough, the American group I was traveling with was comprised of all Catholics. We wondered if this was done by design. You see, while being Caucasian in Poland was not at all out of the ordinary — being Catholic was definitely not unusual. From just our brief stay there (we made four short trips in the course of a year), it was very evident (and interesting!) to see how much the church and the state revolved around each other — even more so than what I had thought in the United States.

The most astonishing thing that happened there was when I went to church for Mass one Sunday morning. The Mass was "said" all in Polish, of which I knew very little (I don't think that knowing how to order a beer is relevant here). Yet, I was able to take in most of what was going on and knew exactly which part of the service the priest was at. The intonation in the priest's voice, the kneeling, the hymns, it was all just as if I was back at my own church — with the added bonus of all of the beautiful stained glass windows!

What was even more amazing was how strongly and devoutly these Polish people followed their faith — at least from what I could tell. All the women had their shoulders covered and many wore a head covering (a veil or hat) too. Everyone was dressed in their "Sunday best." I also noticed that very few people went up for communion, and at first thought that odd. Then I remembered in following our Catholic faith correctly, a person should not be taking of Christ's Body and Blood if he has not recently been to Confession. Thus I assumed (rightly or not) that this was the reason many of the parishioners had chosen not to receive communion that day.

Another thing that struck me during my trips to Poland was that on Sunday mornings, very few stores were open. This too was consistent with my understanding that in a devout Christian community, Sunday was a time for prayer and family. No need to worry — the shops would open later in the day.

My trips to Poland also carried another special blessing since this was where my ancestors are from — my dad, and his family, are 100 percent Polish. My great grandparents were from Krakow. Luckily, I found time the time one weekend to take the train from Warsaw to Krakow and visit the city. While I was there, I walked through the many narrow streets and tiny shops trying to imagine what it was like for my relatives not so many years ago.

My mother, on the other hand, is mostly Irish, with a few relatives from Wales. On this side, I finally got the opportunity to visit Ireland, along with my mom, just this last November. I was so anxious to see where that piece of my heritage belonged — and to see it with my mom made it all the more special! The sheep, the cottages, the clear blue sky — it was just as I had seen in the pictures. I must say the countryside was the most beautiful I have ever seen! I can honestly say — the grass *is* greener there!

Now back to my story. In 1988, I moved to Chicago and met my first husband shortly thereafter, another Catholic. In 1990, we married in a Catholic church and had all the usual Catholic traditions, including attending Pre-Cana (pre-marriage) classes offered by the church. It was a Catholic wedding (yes, with a Mass) and all the praying, kneeling and hymns, etc. It lasted well over an hour.

As it sometimes happens, that marriage did not last — for many reasons not at all related to religion or race. We tried to work things out — after all, divorce was (and still is) a "bad" word in the Catholic faith. Marriage is one of the seven sacraments (along with Baptism, Eucharist/Communion, Reconciliation, Confirmation, Holy Orders and Anointing of the Sick) and I could not and did not take breaking this lightly. In the end, I guess it just wasn't meant to be — for reasons that are not relevant here. But from that marriage, I received a special blessing from God — my one and only child — my daughter, Kimberly.

I will confess that I am not the "best" Catholic in the world. I do attend mass (although not as regularly as I should), I do tithe (give alms to the poor and to the church) and a do have a strong belief in doing what is right for your fellow man — no matter who they are or where they come from. I try not to judge based on color of skin, religious preference or gender. I just really try to accept all people as God's people. We are all here to help each other, and be the best "Christian" (substitute "person") we can be.

Lessons Learned

☪ ✝

We are more than just our own experiences.
Our ancestry plays a role in defining us.

It is possible to show kindness, compassion
and respect regardless of where you
come from or what you believe.

Be open to new cultures — we live
in a wide and diverse world.

CHAPTER 2

How We Met

When I was a kid, I watched a lot of movies. Not surprisingly, it was the rom-coms of the Eighties that shaped my idea of what falling in love was like. I figured if I ever saw a girl the way I watched Kelly LeBrock step out of the closet in *Weird Science* or Phoebe Cates get out of the swimming pool in *Fast Times at Ridgemont High*, I'd know it was the real deal. Of course, reality is a little bit different than the movies and it's not the "lightning strike" moment people expect it to be. So how did I meet Amy? Let's go back to my days in junior high.

There wasn't a week that went by where I wasn't insulted or harassed at school. Whether it was getting the results of a "cool" survey and seeing my name rated dead last to being punched and kicked by a group of boys, there was always something to endure. For years, I begged my parents to enroll me in a martial arts school so I could learn how to defend myself. But try as I might, my father remained totally against the idea.

He'd remind me, gently and patiently, to focus on my grades. Those weren't the words I wanted to hear but over time, I came to understand and respect my father's wisdom. My dream to learn the martial arts never died though. As I grew older, I promised myself that at the very least, my kids would learn how to defend themselves and protect others as well.

When my son, Haroon, turned eight, I enrolled him at the Bruce H. Lee Martial Arts School. He fell in love with Tae Kwon Do immediately and totally immersed himself in training. When his sister, Hassanah, begged me to let her join a few months later, I signed her up too without any reservation. Watching my kids transform into little ninjas, it dawned on me that I could still turn my own dream into a reality. I put my fear and self-doubt to the side and registered myself at the same dojang (Korean for martial arts training hall). I was ready to learn the ancient ways of self-defense.

Master Han Suk Lee (my instructor) taught us that Tae Kwon Do required more than just physical strength and conditioning. The mental attitude and spirit of every martial artist needed to reflect six basic tenets: courtesy, humility, integrity, perseverance, self-control and an indomitable spirit. These traits resonated well with me and with my faith. I might not have understood it in the sixth grade, but being 30 years old, I accepted this quickly and found myself coming more and more into focus every day.

It was also reassuring to know that I wasn't the only middle-aged adult who was serious about martial arts. In fact, half of the students who came to class were over the age of 25. While there were a couple of grown-ups who joined with their kids looking for a "fun family activity," there were about ten of us who were committed to learning Tae Kwon Do for our own benefit. We were a mixed group: African Americans, Caucasians, Indians, Japanese, Koreans and Latinos. Bound together by a common passion and a burning desire to earn our black belts, we quickly and easily became friends.

Master Lee would watch us very carefully in class and would hand-pick only those students he felt were ready to test for their next belt. Little did I know that he had a satellite program at our local park district and students from there would come prepared to sweat it out with the rest of us on testing day. I arrived on a Saturday to test for my green belt and had no idea that my life was about to change.

Amy started Tae Kwon Do as one of "those" grown-ups — the kind looking for a fun family activity. But that Saturday morning, serious-minded and fun-seeking students alike sat on the floor with their backs against the wall as Master Lee began his testing procedures. He started lining up his youngest students first and continued in age order till the last person was called. With over 50 students eagerly waiting to break a board and execute forms, we knew it would be a while before he'd get to the adults. So when Master Lee called on the teenager sitting to my left, I turned to my right and saw a woman smiling very anxiously. I smiled at her and introduced myself. "Hi. I'm Iqbal, like kickball without the K."

"Hi. I'm Amy," she said, and we connected like we were old friends.

I was overly confident that morning — OK, I'll admit it; I was cocky and arrogant that morning. Talking to Amy boosted my confidence a million-fold and definitely took the edge off before our test. It also blurred my judgment and the more we talked, the more I suspected that I would be the last person called on to the mat that morning.

Amy is six years older than me, but there was no way I could have guessed that. With her pleasant smile, youthful eyes and playful nature, I easily pegged her as just having passed the 30-year-old mark. Touting my age like it was a badge of honor, I looked at her and said, "Hmmm. Judging from whose left, I'd say I'll be the last one again." She looked at me, smiled and with a twinkle in her sparkling green eyes, stuck out her hand to accept my challenge. The deal was on! But my puffed up chest deflated in less than two minutes and Amy's smile changed into a very large "I told you so" grin. "Iqbal!" shouted Master Lee, and I solemnly stood and walked over to my place in line. Amy joined me a few seconds later and without saying a word, we smiled at each other silently acknowledging that we had both made a worthy adversary and a good friend.

A few weeks later, Amy left the park district and became a regular at the dojang. We quickly adopted her into our core group and it was only a matter of time until Amy was giving us all a run for our money.

Master Lee would partner me with Amy in class because we shared the same rank and height. With a lot of hard work, sweat and mutual (but constant) motivation, Amy and I became experts at blocking techniques, take downs and forms.

We started Hap Ki Do together, took special classes like Bo staff and Kali sticks (weapons) and even tested together until we had both earned our first-degree black belts. What started out as just two friends supporting each other to reach a common goal turned into a solid partnership built on trust and mutual respect. Her faith and race never factored into anything and I simply accepted her for who she was and how she helped me become better every day.

Our fun wasn't limited to the dojang though. Amy and I and our group of adult martial artists would get together every few months and have some fun! Whether it was a laser-tag party, a summer barbeque, our annual Christmas party or dinner with the black belts, there was plenty of food and plenty of laughs. We all came from different backgrounds and worked in different industries (e.g., government, healthcare, information technology, law enforcement) but it didn't really matter to us. We saw each other as friends and felt comfortable talking with each other and sharing our thoughts, dreams and desires.

One day after class, Amy asked if I could go with her for lunch. She said something was bothering her and she really needed to talk to someone. Call me crazy, but I sensed that it was the first time Amy had asked anyone for help. I agreed and without even changing our uniforms, we drove to Subway, ordered lunch and sat down. She was quiet at first but after some small talk and a few bites of our sandwiches, I asked her, "What's up?" I didn't know what to expect but what I heard definitely took me by surprise.

A few weeks earlier, the black belts from our dojang had organized a clean-up day. We had all arrived that Sunday morning with our families ready to scrub, spray, wipe and vacuum our beloved dojang clean. While most of us were busy cleaning different rooms and taking on different tasks, a senior black belt had secretly cornered Amy and touched her inappropriately. She was at a loss of what to say and what to do but she needed to tell someone. Although I was furious, I knew Amy was a grown-up and she would resolve the issue in a way she found to be comfortable. I offered her a few suggestions and invited her to call me whenever she wanted. It was a huge step forward in our friendship and I could tell she was relieved to just have talked it out.

Things started to change for the both of us after that though. While Tae Kwon Do was important, it wasn't as major as work or family and both were becoming hot topics for us individually. Amy's older brother, Jeff, had suffered a major heart attack and had lost a lot of oxygen to his brain. In a matter of minutes, he had deteriorated from a multi-million dollar economist with VIP clients to a three-year-old child with no memory and no ability to control his own body. Having no one to take care of him, Amy became his legal guardian and flew back and forth to Florida to look after him and handle his affairs.

On the other hand, I had just started my own pharmacy and was spending every waking moment wearing the many entrepreneurial hats of a small business owner. I had put Tae Kwon Do, Toastmasters and all my "extra-curricular" activities on hold and was investing all of my time in advertising, networking and managing my pharmacy, while still working as a full-time pharmacist. It was very time-consuming and I was spending less and less time with my kids.

One day, Amy came to visit me at my store and told me that she and her husband were getting a divorce. I didn't know much about her husband but I knew how stressed she was with her full-time job as an investigator and being Jeff's legal guardian. This was definitely a surprise and I did my best to support her. I told her I was proud of her for taking on so many challenges with grace and gusto. She smiled, but I could tell that she was hurting inside. When she left, I gave her the biggest hug I could and thanked her for coming to see me. That unspoken vibe of trust and friendship hung in the air for days.

My own marriage came to an end a year and a half later. Somewhere during those 17 years, my ex and I had stopped being an authentic

"husband and wife" and I had chosen to ignore it. Only when my pharmacy folded did I realize how busy I had kept myself to avoid the reality
at home. After months of prayer and contemplation, I filed for divorce.
My parents, my children and I moved out of the house that we had
shared for three years and into two new townhomes, built side by side.

Amy and I didn't talk to each other for almost a year, unless you
count funny email forwards as communication. We'd visit the dojang
every once in a while but we were never there at the same time. I was
beginning to miss my friend in a way I couldn't quite describe. I wrestled
with the idea of calling her but I was nervous and afraid I wouldn't know
what to say. After a few weeks of feeling like a sophomore in high school,
I finally sent her an email and asked her if she'd like to meet an old friend
for pizza. I didn't expect to hear from her so quickly but that night, I
checked my email and saw her reply: *Yes!* The light bulb was starting to
brighten over my head but very slowly. I started to connect the dots but
kept wondering, "Am I falling for Amy?"

I arrived first that night at Giordano's Pizza and quickly settled into
our booth. When Amy walked in a few minutes later and made her way
towards me, that's when it hit me! The cheesy Eighties love song started
to play in my head and everything else faded away as she walked in slow
motion. I knew I was in love! Smiling her wonderful Amy smile, she
gave me a big hug and sat down. She looked great! We ordered a pizza
and talked about everything from our jobs, our kids and what we'd been
doing since the last time we saw each other at the dojang. I then asked
how things had been for her since the divorce and since she became her
brother's legal guardian.

Amy never hesitated to share, but there was a distinct sadness in
her tone. I don't know what gave me the courage to do it, but I finally
reached across the table and held her hands. Here she was, pouring out
her heart and all I could do was offer my hands! It took me a while to
notice but after 20 minutes, I realized she hadn't pulled away. Her eyes
and her smile continued to radiate a gentle heat and I knew that there
was something happening between us. She must have felt it too and we

both agreed to meet the following week at a Thai restaurant near her train station. After the second date, I knew she knew too.

We went from one date a week, to two, then three. The more we dated, the more we liked what we saw in each other. The best part was that we were dating and friends. When you start out as friends and then start dating, you get to learn the best parts first before learning the details. As we grew closer and closer, we began to talk openly about our ideals and beliefs. It surprised me to discover how open she was to learning more about Islam and how deeply rooted she was in her own faith at the same time. I may have surprised her with my knowledge of Christianity but through all of our discussions, there was a distinct understanding of how neither of us was looking to convert the other. I knew I was falling in love with her and every day we spent together was another day in paradise.

How We Met

✝

When my daughter, Kim, was young, I enrolled her in various after-school activities. Of course, there were Girl Scouts and swimming lessons, but I was looking for something just a little bit more. Since I was in ballet as a child, I thought "That would be great! Ballet is something every little girl would love to do!" So I signed her up. Well, it didn't go exactly as I'd planned. I'm not sure if she just didn't have the same interest or if it was because class was Friday afternoons, but Kim was just not very happy being in that little pink leotard and slippers. So I had to do some imaginative thinking and decided something a little less "girlie" might be a better choice.

As I scanned through the park district brochure, I came across a kids' class for Tae Kwon Do. This sounded perfect! It would be great exercise, teach her some discipline and it would be fun to do. For the next several weeks, Kim went every Saturday to the park district to learn her new sport. The majority of the time, we both seemed satisfied with her simply taking the class — after all, she was only five years old. After about six months, the instructor convinced me to sign up as well (parents could join for a very low price!). It sounded like a good idea, especially since I was there watching anyway. The next session, Kim and I joined together — each in our brand new white Tae Kwon Do uniform! Although I was only one of three adults, I had a great time learning new skills and practicing basic kicks, blocks and punches with the other kids and their parents.

Near the end of that session, Kim and I decided it was time ... time to begin our journey from white belt to black belt! Our instructor had encouraged us and told us we were ready. The "testing" for our rank belts was offered through the Bruce H. Lee Martial Arts School, one of the local martial arts schools which had co-sponsored the class. Although we had never taken a class at the school, we eagerly (and a bit nervously) got in our uniforms one Saturday morning and went to the "dojang" (the Korean word for training hall).

We walked into the school and were almost overwhelmed by the bright lights, the large blue mat, the wall of mirrors and even the tall shoe rack where we placed our sneakers. We bowed as we "entered" the mat, just as we had been taught during class. Kim and I sat together as we did our stretches, checked our uniforms and got warmed up for the testing. We had an exciting time performing our techniques, reciting our Korean terminology and even breaking boards. Without too much effort, we earned our Yellow belt! My daughter and I agreed that doing Tae Kwon Do was fun and definitely wanted to continue our journey — picturing ourselves one day wearing the sharp black uniform with all the patches *and* that amazing Black Belt with our name on it!

We continued to take classes at the park district once a week, now proudly attending in our white uniforms and new yellow belts. We learned how to do more kicks and improved our techniques — kicking higher and punching harder than ever. Near the end of the next session, we were prepared to test for our next belt level — green this time. Saturday morning we got all dressed — excited about going to the dojang — and readied ourselves for the event. However this time (for me at least), it was different. I found a couple of new interests there on that particular day: I fell in love with training at the dojang, and I met a new friend.

With regard to the training, Master Lee (the head instructor) pulled me to the side and talked to me about coming to the dojang to study so that I could develop at a faster pace than at the park district. At the school, I could also learn from many different instructors, including him. I agreed and shortly thereafter, my daughter and I moved our training and practice to the school. We attended a general class for all ages and belt levels a couple of times a week — usually Saturday mornings and Monday evenings. We both really enjoyed ourselves and our new friends and for me, it was a *great* workout too.

Now, as for my new friends … let's back up to the day of the testing. As was the fashion at this dojang, the students were called to line up in age order — with the youngest at the front. On this particular day, there were about 25 or 30 students, ranging from 5 years old to us "adults." While waiting for our names to be called, we were supposed to remain silent sitting against the back wall. As all of the kids were called up, those of us remaining along the wall dwindled quickly until all that was left was a few of us adults.

I remember vividly, sitting ever so eagerly to get called when I turned and looked at the man sitting next to me. He smiled and said hi. I returned the smile and whispered back. Since they were only about halfway through calling names, we sat patiently and began some quiet chatter (which of course was forbidden in the dojang, but oh well — it was worth the risk). It started with names.

"I'm Amy," I said.

"I'm Iqbal," he said.

"I think I'm going to be called last. I'm the oldest one here," I said.

"No way!" said Iqbal. "I'm older than you!" … and thus began our first argument. Well as it turns out, I am in fact older than Iqbal — but that was just the way our new friendship began.

What was great about the dojang was that once everyone was in uniform (with the exception of the colored belts), everyone was equal. There was no difference in culture or race and certainly no difference in religion. We were all just students learning new skills and techniques and having fun.

To a certain extent, age didn't matter either. Some of the best students were less than half my age and boy, were they amazing to watch! The precision, the power — it brought excitement to my workouts and made me try even harder to be perfect.

Through the dojang, I met several families — some of which had both parents and their children enrolled as students. One of these families was Iqbal's. It was exciting to come to class to see my new friends and to learn new skills. I began to look forward to those Monday nights and Saturday mornings and soon added a Wednesday evening to my schedule.

But there was something more too. I found myself going to the school for the social interaction with the other adults — especially Iqbal. There were sometimes only a few adults in class and because we were about the same height and rank, Iqbal and I partnered up a lot for our drills. In the process, we became even better friends and had some fun times too.

I'll never forget one workout in particular. We were actually doing some Hap Ki Do drills at the time when we were paired up and were literally bending each other's arms around, kicking each other in the stomach and making comments like — "Nope, I don't think that's right — it doesn't hurt." I thought, "How odd to be having this much fun and playing like I was a kid!" I had found a new best friend — someone I could talk to AND roughhouse with! We worked out hard some days and laughed a lot on other days (of course, those were the days we got in trouble and had to do lots of extra pushups). We couldn't help it — it was so much fun!

As our friendship grew, I would look forward to coming to class and finding a spot next to Iqbal. We'd watch ourselves in the mirror to check on the precision of our techniques, but I also found myself catching his eye and smiling. He was always complimenting my toes — of course we were barefoot for class!

While we started in Tae Kwon Do, we then joined Hap Ki Do and even took several classes in weaponry together. I found myself really looking forward to those nights, especially when Iqbal would come to class and we could be partners.

In addition to being friends and sparring partners at the dojang, we also had an occasional lunch together. One of those days, we went to a Subway across the street from the school. We ordered our sandwiches and sat there talking — the next thing I knew almost two hours had gone by! I could have sat there all day talking to him. When we finally walked out to our cars, Iqbal gave me a hug and we agreed we should have lunch together again soon.

Our friendship progressed over time as we attended more classes together and "beat each other up" on more than a few occasions. There was even a session where we were doing Judo throws and, as it happened to be, Iqbal threw his partner at precisely the same time my partner threw me. I had landed first and was still on my back when Iqbal's partner's foot came crashing down directly onto my mouth! I was knocked out, literally! When I came to a few minutes later, the whole class was standing over me and all I could say through my new fat lip and loose teeth was "What happened?" Don't worry — I eventually healed, but I teased Iqbal for quite a while about that day.

My journey towards that magnificent Black Belt continued with both Iqbal and I attending class when we could and moving up in rank one colored belt at a time. All the while, our friendship continued to grow.

During the next couple of years, the road of life took a few hard turns including my getting divorced and dealing with some pretty serious family issues. Luckily, Iqbal was there as a constant and faithful friend. We chatted at various times over the phone, via computer and even in person. He was an endless reminder of what a good listener and a real friend could be.

Then one day, things changed … again! Iqbal asked me to go out for pizza to catch up as old friends do. He had been busy and had not been able to make it to the dojang for quite some time. We agreed and planned on meeting at Giordano's Pizza the following week.

As I was getting ready for what I now realize was actually a date, I felt excited and nervous at the same time. "But why?" I thought to myself. "I've known Iqbal for years and we've talked hundreds of times." Well, that night was different. We ate pizza, talked and laughed. At one point in the conversation, however, things got a bit more serious. We talked about the difficulties I was having in my personal life. In retrospect, I realize this was just due to "life" taking its twists and turns but at the time, it felt more like I was on a roller coaster — both physically and emotionally. As I was venting my frustrations and my concerns, Iqbal reached out across the table and held my hands. I was surprised but yet, I didn't move. I felt comfort from him in both the touch of his hands and the love I could see in his eyes. There was genuine friendship, trust and love revealed that night — and my heart swelled.

What was even more interesting (as I think back on it now) was that at no time did I stop and think, "Wow! Iqbal's brown and he's Muslim." It never even occurred to me that he was any different than I was — except of course that he was a man. Neither race nor religion entered into my head when we began our friendship. Sure, I could tell by the color of his skin that he was darker than I am — that was obvious. But I never thought of him as being any different than me.

After many hours of talking, I found that we had the same basic principles in life, the same general philosophies and the same set of beliefs. I think I knew somewhere along the line that he was a Muslim, but did it really matter? Not in a friendship such as ours! We were true friends who could discuss anything and just enjoyed doing things together.

That reminds me of another quick story. Remember when I said I am both a wife *and* a friend? Well, one night when Iqbal and I were having a rather serious discussion about life, I told him that I loved having him as a friend and that I hoped we would always be friends. That seemed like a pretty logical and complimentary thing for me to say, especially at that phase of our relationship.

However, the response I received was rather shocking at first and certainly *not* what I had expected. "I don't want to be your friend," Iqbal

said very matter-of-factly. I sat there across from him just dumbfounded!
Here I was thinking that we were moving forward with our relationship
— actually hoping we were — and then he hits me with that?! After my
initial stunned expression passed, I whimpered, "But why?" to which he
replied, "I want to be more than that."

From there our discussion got even stranger. I attempted to explain
my belief that to be together as anything more still meant that we had to
be friends. It was a baseline for me and every relationship should build
up from there — friendship should *never* go away. From Iqbal's point of
view it seemed that two people, who were thinking of being together as
husband and wife, could no longer be friends — but rather a married
couple. After several more discussions, we found that our thoughts were
actually the same but that our definitions were different. His definition
of a husband–wife relationship encompassed all the same virtues and
values that mine did *plus* those of my term friends! We were thinking
the same thing — it just didn't sound that way at first. Thus a new lesson
learned — always be sure to clarify and explain your point of view. I
could have just as easily shut down at that point that he said, "I don't
want to be your friend." After all, it might seem to be a very hurtful statement when in fact, it was just the opposite!

As our friendship grew and our dating continued, we also began
to discuss the differences in our faiths and our cultures. It was interesting for me to learn that so much of what I had assumed about Iqbal
was based on his Muslim faith rather than his Indian/Pakistani culture.
Some of these differences are still difficult for me to understand, but I
keep trying.

One of these conversations took place the evening when we decided
to visit the Baha'i Temple in Wilmette, Illinois. During our drive, I
began to ask Iqbal all those questions that I had always wondered about
Muslims but perhaps been afraid to ask. While many of the subjects
will be discussed in later chapters of this book, the point I want to make
is that once you find a friend who can be open to you and you to them,
the world is then at your fingertips. I could ask Iqbal anything — and
I mean anything — related to Islam. My main questions were all those

"why's"? Why do women wear the hijab? Why do men and women not sit together at masjid (the term for prayer hall)? Why do Muslim men place women as second-class citizens and not as equals?

As you will soon see, Iqbal answered these questions and more in great detail. Now, I too am able to understand (sometimes) and respect (always) his faith and culture, although I don't necessarily agree with various parts. Perhaps some of my reluctance to simply believe and accept his views is based on the way I was raised (Catholic and American) or perhaps it is just who I am.

Lessons Learned

Smile! It brings joy and peace.

In disagreements, explain your position clearly
— you may be meaning the same thing.

People we meet on a journey can change our lives.

You never know where good friends can be found.

When you comfort someone, just
let your heart do the talking.

Chapter 3

Meeting the Family

Amy and I found ourselves spending every spare moment we could with each other. Being a pharmacist, this might be heresy for me to say, but it felt like I was on drugs — the good kind! Every smile, every glance, every new discovery about Amy was a new "high" for me and that "floating" feeling lasted for days. One day, I found a sheet of paper on her desk with multiple attempts at a new signature — Amy K. Atcha! It took me three weeks to wipe the grin off my face. As we grew closer, I decided it was time to share the news with my friends and family. Family members are people you love because you have to, but friends are people you love because you choose to. I decided to start with my friends first.

There's a beautiful poem on the Internet, author unknown, about friends called, "A Reason, a Season or a Lifetime." It talks about friends who come into your life for a reason or a season. They stay for a short time and help you solve a problem or grow in some way and then they leave. Some of my friends "for a reason and a season" stayed with me until I was divorced and then we parted ways. I'll always be grateful for the support they gave me but the poem also talks about "friends for a lifetime." These are friends who stay with you through thick and thin. They don't call you every day but you can still pick up the phone months (even years) later and nothing's changed. They'll stop traffic for you and they'll be there in a split second whenever you need them. My friends for a lifetime are Adnan, Irfan, Mayur and Naveed. They've known me for decades and have been a source of strength for me during many life events. They're my brothers and they were the ones I went to first with the news.

I invited them to dinner one night at Big Bowl in Schaumburg. We hadn't seen each other in a few months and I wanted tell my "bros" (that's slang for brothers) face-to-face. When I told them I was seeing Amy, an Irish-Polish Catholic, they didn't even blink. Like true brothers, all they saw was that I was in love and that I was at peace. The only question they had was when they'd get to meet her. So, I promised them they'd get to grill Amy in person at my summer barbecue (pun intended). It felt good to be loved and accepted but I was already strategizing how to tell the next group: my kids. This was going to be a little harder.

Haroon (my son) and Hassanah (my daughter) had gotten to know Amy over the years through Tae Kwon Do. They had trained with her and had hung out with her and Kim (Amy's daughter) at plenty of events. I knew they saw her as a respected elder and someone they could trust. So why was I nervous about telling them she and I had gone from "just friends" to something more? The truth was that I was afraid that they wouldn't accept Amy as a stepmother.

Part of my fear stemmed from what other parents had shared with me about their teenagers when they were in the same situation. If you've ever heard the dreaded phrase, "She's not my *real* mom," you know what I mean. Both of my kids were in their teens/pre-teens and Haroon was showing signs of teen angst pretty regularly. The other reason was because Amy wasn't Muslim and wasn't going to become one. Islam was a daily part of Haroon's and Hassanah's lives and the Islamic environment they had grown up in had defined their upbringing up to that point. I wasn't sure how introducing a non-Muslim as a parental figure into their life was going to change that.

Like most kids, Haroon and Hassanah had a daily afterschool routine. They followed the same marching orders that probably every parent around the world gives their kids: clean your room, do your homework, wash your hands, set the dinner table and take out the trash. After dinner, they'd get ready for bed and I'd check to see how well they washed their faces and brushed their teeth. But being Muslim, we also prayed together every night and they spent an hour reading and discussing the Quran with either my father (Dada) or my mother (Dadi). Every morning, we'd pray, have breakfast and would practice reciting parts of the Quran (called surahs) on our drive to school. Once we finished our chores and prayers on the weekends, we'd go sledding, bike riding or hiking in a forest or nature preserve. We had blended both our religious life and our everyday life into a perfect routine. I just didn't know how things would play out after this.

So Amy and I decided that it would be best if our kids "watched" our relationship progress first hand. This took a bit of work and our initial "family dates" weren't as impromptu as the kids might believe. A couple of days beforehand, we mapped out a strategy and decided that Amy and Kim would arrive at the movie theater first. Then we'd arrive ten minutes later and run into each other. After saying hi, we'd discover that we were both headed in to see the same movie (*surprise! surprise!*).

With all five of us sitting in the same row, it gave Amy and me the perfect opportunity to hold hands in the dark but also to observe how well (or not) the kids got along. We saw the "big brothers are too cool for little sisters" phenomenon and the "sisters are best friends" syndrome prominently on display. It was a good start to say the least.

As the weeks turned into months, our play-dates transformed from "random collisions" to planned outings and group activities. The girls adjusted to each other pretty quickly and soon, we were one big happy family ... almost. Haroon remained distant with everyone and everything. I chalked it up to "teen angst," and even though he came with us everywhere and did exactly what we did, he was just mopey all the time. We did our best not to notice and just accepted it for what it was.

We'd gotten very comfortable with each other and the kids had gotten used to us dating (even though we never used those exact words). Amy and I were moving steadily towards marriage and I kept thinking

about the right way to tell Haroon and Hassanah. I wanted to be direct
but gentle. It wasn't that I needed their approval, but it would've been
nice. One Saturday afternoon, I took them to Mallard Lake Forest
Preserve for one of our nature walks. We were quiet for a long while
and after a few miles in, I asked them what they thought about Amy and
Kim. I kept hoping they would be completely honest with me and I had
prepared myself to listen like never before.

With a huge smile, Hassanah started to ramble on and on about
how much she enjoyed spending time with them. "It's like having another
sister!" exclaimed Hassanah. She called Amy "step-mom" twice before
stopping in her tracks and asking "Abbu (Dad), are you going to ask her
to marry you?"

Perfect lead-in! "Yes," I said. "What do you think about that?"

That's when Haroon finally spoke. "I don't like it."

He didn't say it like he was mad, but you could see hurt and resentment on his face. I wasn't 100 percent sure but I thought I knew why.
Raising him Muslim, I had repeatedly stressed the importance our faith
places in loving one's mother. Blessed with the responsibility of carrying,
delivering, nursing, and raising children, moms are the strongest pillar of
the family and are typically a child's first (and best) teacher of ethics and
values. There's a hadith (story) in which Prophet Muhammad (peace be
upon him) instructed Muslims to love and respect their mother so highly
that she should be first, second *and* third in a person's life. That's not to
say that a father's role isn't as meaningful. His wisdom and strength are
crucial as well, but it's the mom who gives all of herself (both physically
and emotionally) to her child's growth and development.

Haroon had always been a mild-mannered kid and he'd never gotten
upset over anything before. But I could tell that this conversation was
different. He saw my decision to marry Amy as a threat to his feelings of
love, protection and loyalty for his mother. I wasn't fully prepared for that
head on collision, but I wasn't going to quit until he understood my perspective. I kept praying to Allah to let me sound calm, cool and collected.

We were standing on a bridge overlooking a lake when our conversation had come to an abrupt stop. Haroon's words hung in the air but instead of fighting an uncomfortable silence, I found myself in a state of serenity. Call it "divine intervention" or just call me crazy, but it felt like God was answering my prayers and giving me peace of mind. I could feel the sun's rays warm my neck and back and I could hear the sound of the waves below us lapping against the bridge in perfect harmony.

With nature's serenity as my guide, I inhaled deeply and explained that Amy wasn't going to replace his mother. Instead, Amy would be an addition to our family. Very solemnly and quietly, Hassanah asked if she was going to become Muslim. "No." I said. "Neither of us is going to change who we are for the sake of the other. She'll continue to practice her faith and we'll continue to practice ours." It was those final words that broke the tension. I had braced myself for some snotty teenager comeback but instead, I received a hug from Hassanah and a very bland "OK" from Haroon.

Most people think that it must've been the hardest thing to tell my kids the news. In all honesty, telling them was easy. It was sharing the news with my parents that I dreaded. I had lived with my parents under the same roof (or next door) ever since I was born. In most Asian cultures, it's rare for a son to move away from their parents. When a new job or a new wife enters the picture, the family goes and grows together. In Indo-Pak and most Asian cultures, it goes without saying that the sons (primarily) take care of their aging parents. My brother, who is five years older than me, had moved to Florida to raise his own family and had no plans to move back. I had prepared myself to be their caretaker from a very young age and it wasn't going to change now.

When I got divorced, I decided to sell the "big house" (the home where we had all lived together) and to find something close by, but separate. We found two new townhomes next door to each other that were still under construction and bought them on the spot. Amy and I had started dating a few months after this when we finally closed the deal and my parents and I moved in. They had met Amy many years ago at the dojang but she was just a friend back then. Now, they were watching her Ford Escape pull into my driveway one or two evenings a week and they weren't too happy about it.

My father was an "elder" in our community and had counseled many family members and friends over the years. When it came to marriage, he was simple but direct — marry only within our culture and only within our religion. It was a concept that resonated with everyone in our family — everyone, that is, but me and my brother. I knew that my parents were smart and they had to know I was dating someone, but I don't think they knew it was a divorced, white, Christian!

I still had dinner with my parents every night when I wasn't at work. They never asked me about my love-life or about the blue Ford Escape, but their silence was disapproval enough. I got the feeling that they wanted to avoid the topic altogether, hoping that might make the issue go away. I had been looking for the "right way" to break the news to them but I had chickened out before trying. It was the end of summer when "the breakdown" finally happened. The moment of truth arrived one evening when I came home from work and started watering my lawn.

I had stood on my lawn for just a few minutes before my father came outside to water his grass as well. I smiled, waiting for him to turn around and wave, but he never did. I waited and waited and waited, but after 15 minutes, I knew that my father was done with me. This was his ultimate display of disapproval and I took it to mean, "We won't speak with you until you stop what you are doing and come to your senses." The feeling was mutual and we made a silent agreement in that moment to part ways. The next day, all communication with my mom and my extended family came to a stop as well. My aunts, uncles and cousins around the world had heard what was happening and out of respect for my father, they stopped talking to me. Only my brother and a handful of cousins were able to look past my "transgression" and kept in contact with me. It would be another three years before my parents and I would speak again.

Meeting the Family

✝

As Iqbal and I continued to date, we decided it was only fair to let our children know that our relationship had gone beyond the "family friends" stage. As we might have guessed, the kids were initially delighted. The girls (both Hassanah and Kim) were happy when they realized that they would have a sister. Kim also had the pleasure of gaining the new big brother she had always wanted. The kids saw this union simply as an extension to an already close friendship.

The rest of Iqbal's family, however, was not as enchanted. In fact, some might say they were downright *un*happy. Before Iqbal's parents knew that we were "dating," they were very pleasant. They would say their hellos and goodbyes when I happened to be at his house. Iqbal, who was actually living with his parents (as is customary in his culture) found it a bit harder to deal with. His mother asked him on several occasions where he was going and what he was doing but I don't think he told them the whole story — especially the part about me being Catholic!

A few months later when he came out and told them directly about our relationship, I sensed that there was a lot of tension. I no longer visited his house and sadly, my contact with his family involved only Iqbal and his children. This was a new and strange experience for me, seeing as Iqbal had quite a bit of extended family in the area. Simply because I was white and Christian, I was not welcome in Iqbal's family home, nor were we welcome to join in at parties and gatherings of other family members. You might say we were "shunned."

My family, on the other hand, was actually rather un-opinionated. Having been married to a white Catholic before and that relationship not having ended well, I guess my mom thought, "What's the harm?" Both Mom and Dad asked a lot of questions (and still do to this day) about Iqbal, his family and his faith. They too, have made their share of inappropriate comments — not purposefully mean, but rather just due to ignorance or based on the stereotypes that they had heard. In the early days, I spent a great deal of time explaining to them the whys and whats that I had learned. As a result, I have found that stereotyping is an extremely poor way of gaining wisdom about the world.

My friends' reactions to my relationship with Iqbal also varied. My closest friends saw past both the race and religious issues and remarked that we looked like two people who had fallen madly in love and seemingly were made for each other. Besides, the more they got to know Iqbal, the less the color of his skin and his religion really seemed to matter. It was only his name that would tend to trip people up! But even with my dearest friends, they too had questions about Islam and the Indo-Pak culture. Thankfully, they felt comfortable asking me, wanting simply to learn and not show any negativity towards me or Iqbal.

Other friends, however, did not act this way. I had one friend in particular that, to this day, thinks that all Muslims are "bad" or "evil." Perhaps it is the perpetual drama which exists subsequent to 9/11. Just as many racist people do, he chose not to look past the color of Iqbal's skin or his religious views. Unfortunately (or maybe not), our friendship has run its course mostly because I choose to only associate with people who are tolerant of other people's beliefs. My perspective is that I don't always have to agree with everyone, but I do need to respect them.

Back to our story. For the first three years of my relationship with Iqbal, he spent a great deal of time getting to know my parents and brothers. My family is spread throughout the world — literally. Mom is in Tennessee, Dad and his wife Sue live in Ohio, my brother Dan and his family live in Texas, and my brother Matt and his family currently live in London and are on their way to Australia. I don't speak to my brothers too often but I'm in contact with Mom and Dad on a biweekly basis.

The news of my engagement to Iqbal was shared with my Mom almost immediately, with my Dad and my brothers shortly thereafter.

They wanted to know all about Iqbal and, of course, my mom wanted the full scoop on his family as well. I tried to share as much as I thought they could absorb at any one time. To share everything about a person in one sitting can be rather overwhelming, especially someone I had known for almost eight years! Nonetheless, I shared with my family snippets of our friendship, our dating, Iqbal's faith and his culture. Watching my family learn about him (and Iqbal learn about them) was like watching a heart-warming romance movie — with each side gaining more insight and sharing more love with every new detail. (Awwww!)

Unfortunately, Iqbal and I spent an equal amount of time those first several years *avoiding* his parents. Not to place blame, but it really wasn't my doing. His parents were apparently not at all happy with his decision to marry me — and they let us know it! At first, I was only mildly uncomfortable not having any type of relationship with Iqbal's parents. But then the frustration began to grow with each passing day.

Did I mention that we live next door to them? The proximity of our houses made for some very awkward situations and as the days went on, just that simple fact added to the tension. I should add that Iqbal's parents weren't speaking with him at all either. From my understanding, he had "shamed" the family with his divorce and then made matters worse by marrying a white girl, and a Catholic at that. While this feeling of resentment from his parents was very disheartening, I knew that it was not a new concept. Many interfaith and interracial couples face this same predicament — however, it was a first for me.

When I moved into our house, I would look at his parents' house and wonder, "Why don't they like me? They don't even really know me." But as the weeks went by and their disapproval became more and more apparent, the frustration turned to anger! "How dare they not speak to me!" I thought. "I'll show them!" During the next several months, both Iqbal's parents and I would carefully and purposefully avoid each other — no eye contact, no signs of recognition, not even a simple neighborly wave.

At some point, I realized how ridiculous this all was! We were family — whether we liked it or not! "We could at least be neighborly," I said to myself and to Iqbal as well. I urged him to contact his parents, particularly his mom — he was closer to her than to his dad and it would seem she was much less upset too — just to let them know we were here and that they were loved. If they wanted to reciprocate, it would be their choice. Next came the mailing of birthday cards, anniversary cards and Christmas cards (perhaps this was a thorn in their sides?). Then, we went on to send a holiday/fall poinsettia plant and some spring flowers. Silly as it may seem, we actually mailed the cards and flowers to them even though they merely lived next door.

Although for months (dare I say years) it seemed that all our efforts were in vain. Still we persisted and I kept thinking, "If they don't want to have a relationship with me, then fine, but I am *not* going to stop trying!" Iqbal too continued his calls (actually messages) to his mom as well. Sometimes, we even pulled out all the stops and sent the kids over with "peace offerings" to share when we baked cookies or made a large dinner. Surely they wouldn't refuse their own grandchildren!

Then one sunny afternoon, about three years into our marriage, the doorbell rang. It was Iqbal's mom, Zulekha! Needless to say, Iqbal and I were in shock and *very* pleasantly surprised. From that point forward our relationship grew. Although it took a few more months for Iqbal's dad (Ismail) to "come around," we definitely repaired our relationship and continue to learn much from and about each other every day.

Whether it's my imagination or not, the first signs of love and caring from Iqbal's dad came when he gave me a flu shot. He also shared with me a book on Mary, the mother of Jesus, and her importance in Islam. In return, I gave both Ismail and Zulekha some gifts I had chosen for them from the Islamic Center in Washington, D.C. (I had been there recently on a work trip). These gifts were graciously given and received and were the first of many signs of sharing the mutual respect we have for each other's faiths and beliefs. It never fails to amaze me but gifts and food are the universal language of acceptance, tolerance, politeness and respect.

We are still getting to know each other now — especially in learning family traditions. I am learning how to cook some Indian/Pakistani dishes and we are continually sharing our food — a watermelon is just too much for a family of two to eat in a week. I am learning that spices are the key and the only real difference in the way we cook — but what a difference it makes!

My mom did not meet Iqbal's parents until almost a year later and my dad only just met Ismail and Zulekha this past summer. The meetings between the two families brought with it the typical anxiety of any couple — will the parents have anything to talk about? Will they embarrass me? But ours was even more challenging since Iqbal and I were *already* married and for well over three years!

Both events (meeting my mom and meeting my dad) were very much the typical in-law exchanges. There was the awkward small talk over appetizers while we all sat around the coffee table. But the longer we all sat together, the more the parents began carrying on their own conversations, seemingly ignoring Iqbal and me. To our great relief, there were no fist-fights, no name-calling, and no opposition as a result of the different religions and different cultures. Due to the distance between their houses, they don't see each other often, but frequently ask about the other and seem to genuinely care about each other's well-being. It's nice to know that there is no hostility between the families and I'm certain that when there is another opportunity to all gather together, we will all pleasantly socialize and mingle.

The winds of change are still blowing as I begin to meet and interact with the rest of Iqbal's extended family. It was only this past year — four years into our marriage — that we invited Iqbal's entire family to attend a party at our house. Iqbal's aunts, uncles and cousins came from all over the Chicagoland area and we all had a really nice time — at least from my perspective. That night at the party, I even learned how to make Chai! I remember smiling from ear to ear while sipping some tea — I finally felt that I had been accepted!

Happily now, when I see Zulekha and Ismail, we wave to each other or sometimes stop by for a quick hello. It is encouraging and wonderful that we speak (at least weekly) and share in the small things as well as the big events. I am also blessed that they are reciprocating that love with hugs and well wishes when we visit. When we part ways, they have taught me to say, "Allah Hafiz," which loosely translated means "May God be your Guardian." What a great and universal way to show we care!

Lessons Learned

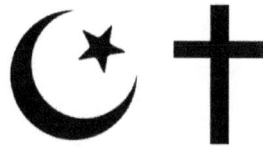

☪ ✝

Building and maintaining family
relationships takes energy and work.

Parents rarely see things the same way
as their kids (and vice-versa).

Your real friends just want you to be happy.

Gifts and food are the universal language of
acceptance, tolerance, politeness, and respect.

CHAPTER 4

Our Wedding

Even though I had known Amy for years, I didn't know a lot about her. In fact, our first date at Giordano's was the first time she had really opened up to me about her life. I had no idea how well she got along with her family, what her spending habits were or what made her happy — but I was determined to find out. Every date became a Q&A session for the both of us and we opened up about our beliefs, our values, and our histories. We learned about each other's childhood, the steps (and missteps) we took during college, our successes and failures and our hopes and dreams.

We did a lot of sharing over dinner and we visited a lot of Indian and Asian restaurants. Don't get me wrong, we visited plenty of steakhouses and burger joints as well. But being Indian/Pakistani and a really big "foodie," I wanted Amy to experience the sights, smells and tastes of my childhood. One of our very first dates was at India Garden in Westmont. She had never eaten Indian food before and I ordered a few traditional dishes to get us started. After a few bites, I looked over to see a very puzzled Amy. "Where's the silverware?" she asked. It had slipped my mind to tell her that in most Eastern cultures, we eat with our hands. So instead, I tore off a piece of naan (bread), scooped up some mutter paneer (peas and cottage cheese) and placed it in her mouth. It didn't escape our attention that eating Indian food can be a romantic experience!

All of our dates were special, but not all of our dates involved food. We had a couple of serious ones as well. One of our more enlightening dates was at the Baha'i House of Worship in Wilmette. It was a place my parents had taken me to when I was a little boy and I had fallen in love with its architecture and botanical gardens. The place emitted a deep sense of peace and tranquility and I knew Amy would love it as much as I did. We spent an entire day at the temple learning about the Baha'i faith, listening to a service and exploring the similarities between world religions. Our ride home was filled with discussions about Islam and Christianity, the tenets of our respective faith and how everyone (regardless of culture or faith) longs for peace. It was a very deep conversation and it was a watershed moment for me.

Though we didn't practice our love for Allah the same way, we both loved the Creator and we both strived for His love in return. We saw a connection between ourselves, God and the people around the world. Every moment we spent together (as a couple or as a family) strengthened the bond between us. The more we dated, the more I knew Allah had brought her into my life for a reason. I knew I wanted her to be my wife and having shared my intentions with Haroon and Hassanah, I was ready to pop the question.

My friends weren't sure why I wanted to get married again, but my reasons were simple and clear. I wanted Amy to see how serious I was about her. I wanted to be with her for richer or for poorer, for better or for worse, in sickness and in health till death do us part. It was also important to both of because of our faiths. Both Christianity and Islam see marriage as something holy, pure and essential to being a good believer.

Christians see it as one of the seven sacraments and Muslims believe that getting married (and raising a family) fulfills half of one's religious duties. It's the ultimate expression of love, honor and commitment. Making a promise to God in front of family and friends was the best way I knew to honor Allah for His blessing and to continue to receive more. We also wanted to set a good example for our kids and we hoped that our marriage would serve as another reminder. It was an expectation we had of them and what they should expect of themselves when they grew up and became responsible adults.

As an American-Muslim, I wanted my proposal (and my wedding) to combine the best of both worlds. Every wedding I've ever attended had a religious part and a cultural part, but determining where the two start and finish was a mystery. My faith meant a lot to me and I was determined to incorporate what I could into my wedding. Thank Allah for the Internet!

I did some research and discovered that there were four major requirements for an Islamic marriage:

1. A clear proposal

2. A clear acceptance

3. At least two competent witnesses present at the wedding

4. A gift from the groom to the bride

What a relief! This was pretty simple stuff. While it looked like a no-brainer in today's day and age, the rules of an Islamic marriage were created at a time when things were very different.

Back in 600 A.D., marriages in Arab *and* European countries were based on feudal and patriarchal laws. More often than not, this forced couples together in the name of loyalty or political gain. Islamic law did away with that and made it so that neither the bride nor the groom could be forced into a marriage without their full consent. Both a man and a woman had the right to say no and with two witnesses present, not even the strongest willed parent could override their decision. The gift to the bride (commonly referred to back then as dowry) was a token of love from her new husband. It wasn't a fee or a price-tag for "buying her" as some people claim. It belonged solely to the wife (upon acceptance of the marriage proposal) and could be enjoyed by her and her alone.

With these stipulations in mind, I started to get things in order. The first thing I needed was "the gift." Choosing the right engagement ring wasn't going to be easy — especially for Amy! Judy, Amy's mother, had told how exacting her daughter was, especially when it came to jewelry. Unless Amy had a say in it, I knew she wouldn't have been happy so Amy and I spent a few weeks walking through 3 shopping malls and 20 different jewelry stores. We looked at rings of all cuts, shapes and sizes and I kept reminding myself (especially when I'd get frustrated) that getting her input was priceless. After several visits to Whitehall Jewelers, I stopped by one day after work and bought "the one."

I was now ready and pumped for Phase Two: the proposal! In Indian and Pakistani cultures, it's tradition for the groom's parents to bring a proposal to the bride's parents and ask them for the daughter's hand in marriage. Needless to say, Amy isn't Indian or Pakistani and I wasn't on speaking terms with my parents. Besides, this wasn't something I identified with. I was a first-generation Indo-Pak who had watched enough TV to know what an American proposal should look like. The question wasn't how to do it, but if could I pull it off!

The maître d' at Nick's Fish Market in Rosemont, Ilinois, was more than willing to help. I sent him my list of ideas to make the night as magical as possible and he was on board. Amy and I had never eaten at a seafood restaurant before and she was excited to try something new. After they seated us, the maître d' began to send each member of his staff over to our table every ten minutes. As they approached, they would stop, lay a beautiful red rose next to her and say, "A beautiful rose for a beautiful lady." As each rose was laid next to Amy, the eyes of the restaurant's patrons, the wait staff and Amy's grew bigger and bigger.

After she had received a dozen roses, the maître d' wheeled the dessert cart to our table. He began telling us about the restaurant's special menu — chocolate cake, caramel pecan pie, etc. His spiel sounded rather blah and it was the perfect disguise because Amy didn't see it coming! When he lifted the silver dome off the dessert cart to present the "house specialty," there sat a 1.25-carat Marquise-cut diamond, set in white gold, on a bed of ice. I have to tell you, it's probably the only time I've ever seen Amy speechless! Her jaw dropped and she began to wave her hands wildly in front of her face. To top it all off, she started to hyperventilate — I mean seriously hyperventilate! I wasn't sure if I should continue or call an ambulance but I had come this far and with my "witnesses" in the restaurant watching, I couldn't ruin the moment.

I got down on one knee and poured out my heart to her. I kept waiting for her to calm down and start breathing but she was still waving her hands like she was ready to fly. When I asked her, "Will you marry me?" there was no answer. What seemed like 5 minutes of silence was probably 60 seconds, and I had to repeat my question again. I was beginning to think she had really gone into shock and we might actually have to call the ambulance. Finally, she gasped and said, "Yes!" Whew! I wasn't sure what to expect on our wedding day but I prayed it would be nothing like this!

With our wedding date set for January, we now had to answer the big question — what type of wedding would we have? At first, we talked about having three different kinds: one Islamic, one Catholic and one secular. Not having fully discussed it, we thought this option would make each other happy and help satisfy our own spiritual/cultural sides as well. But after some lengthy conversations, we realized that neither of us wanted to get married inside a mosque or a church and neither of us wanted an Imam or a Catholic priest to officiate the ceremony. Working together, we found elements of both faiths that were essential to us and decided that we could have one ceremony after all.

Finding someone to officiate our wedding wasn't as big of a challenge either. We contacted clergymen of several faiths that had conducted interfaith weddings before and we picked a Methodist pastor to marry us. This may seem odd at first, but the reason why was simple: he agreed to use God instead of Jesus or Allah throughout the ceremony. Amy and I found common ground in all areas of planning our wedding. Neither of us wanted to be dictated by cultural traditions or religious doctrine and we wanted the ceremony to be performed to our specifications. Our next stop was to find a wedding hall and after a few quick searches, the holy grail of places appeared — the Embassy Suites Chicago in Oak Brook, Illinois.

From the moment we stepped inside the atrium, its rivers with koi fish and lush vegetation took us instantly back to the Baha'i House of Worship. Tranquility and peace surrounded us both and the garden paradise resembled our vision of heaven. It didn't take us long after that to take care of the bridal gown, tuxedo rentals, catering, deejay, etc., and we eagerly counted down the days to January 13, 2007.

The wedding was exactly how I had pictured it, except in one way. My parents and I had not made our peace yet and I decided not to invite them. I knew my parents wouldn't accept my marriage and that they would not want to witness their son involved in a "Christian" marriage (i.e., not an Indo-Pak Muslim ceremony). I was a little shocked that my brother, sensing the tension in the family, decided not to come, but I understood that it was his way of honoring my father. On the groom's side, a total of seven guests (including Mayur, Adnan and Irfan) were there to witness my marriage.

On the big day, Haroon (my best man) and I donned our purple and silver tuxedos and stood at the altar. It was exciting and humbling at the same time knowing that Amy would soon be signing her name for real the way she did on that sheet of paper I found. As the harpist began to play the Wedding March, Hassanah and Kim preceded walking Amy down the aisle. The pastor's sermon dripped with words of love and encouragement and there was an overall sense of joy and humility. Amy and I did keep one element of a Christian wedding: we both lit a unity candle.

While it's common in most Catholic weddings, we decided not to blow out our individual candles and let them burn alongside the new one to symbolize that our individual characteristics would remain. When the pastor pronounced us man and wife, I kissed the bride and heard 200 people — our friends, family *and* the hotel guests from the floors above — clapping and congratulating us. It was a moment I'll never forget.

Our Wedding

✝

After several months of sharing dinners, watching movies and attending some bigger events, Iqbal and I began thinking that we should spend the rest of our lives together ... we should tie the knot ... we should get married! Now don't get me wrong, we knew that not every day was going to be full just of the "fun and games" we had been having, but we were ready to tackle life hand in hand.

After the initial giddiness and delight of realizing I had a true Best Friend Forever (BFF), the reality of a life-long commitment began to set in. Before I could move forward with the notion of our wedding and a life together though, Iqbal and I needed to have a serious talk. Not just about who would handle the finances or who would clean the house — but about something much more sensitive and personal ... religion and culture.

Up to this point, I had spent some time learning about Islam and the Indian/Pakistani culture primarily through Iqbal. Throughout this learning, I was constantly comparing what he had taught me to Catholicism and my American way (with a few Irish and Polish customs thrown in). But now, we were at a different point in our relationship — that of actually "living" with each other's practices and beliefs — and it started with a discussion of the wedding itself.

Although Iqbal had not officially "popped the question," we felt as if we needed to have some discussions about how exactly our life would look together and just how we would be able to incorporate Islam and

Catholicism into our marriage. I was very adamant that I was *not* going to convert to Islam and likewise, Iqbal was very definite about his desire to continue with his faith. We had several talks while walking through Cantigny Park, the local forest preserves and over coffee. From each of these chats, I realized that I really *did* have a strong connection to my faith and that no amount of compromise was going to make me see differently. I got the same feeling from Iqbal.

Then, as if lightning had struck, we realized that we did *not* need to combine the two, but rather that we should celebrate in them both! Why not share the love of God in both ways — mine still through Catholicism and his through Islam?

Our wedding was our first example of this new dual-religious life together (note that I did say "dual," not "duel"). During the next several hours of talking and brainstorming, we sifted through the possibilities for the wedding, thinking maybe we would have two ceremonies — one Catholic and one Islamic — or have just a civil type of ceremony with no religious aspect. But these ideas just didn't seem to resonate.

Again, lightning struck! Why not have one single wedding with elements of both faiths? It would be a true blending of not only ourselves, but of our families and our lives.

Now that the hard part had been decided, next we needed to find a venue. We thought briefly about the possibility of having the wedding at the Baha'i Temple, since we had really enjoyed it when we visited earlier that year. It seemed like the perfect spot since the Baha'i teachings emphasize that all of us (as creations of one God) are part of one human family. They acknowledge that there are several religions in the world, each emphasizing a specific Messenger sent from above. The Baha'i believe that these religions come from the same Source and are (in essence) successive chapters of one religion from God.

While this all seemed fine, in the end we decided it wasn't quite the right thing to do. We did not want to subscribe to a new way of thinking but rather truly relish in the blending of our own steadfast religions.

We began to look around at some other sites, including Chicago's beautiful Botanical Gardens. We had decided early on that we did not want to have our wedding in either a church or a mosque, mainly to alleviate any bias or confusion. It truly was to be a union of two equal partners, each in their own faith and under one God. Instead, we chose to be married in the atrium of the Embassy Suites in Oakbrook, Illinois. The hotel had a beautiful, lush, garden-type atmosphere with a large open gazebo in the center. We decorated the area with purple and white flowers and silk cloths and with the existing greenery, it made for the perfect picture.

Knowing that neither a Catholic priest nor an Imam would marry us without both of us being of that same faith, we decided instead to have a non-denominational minister perform our vows. We met with him on a couple of occasions to get to know him as he was learning about us. We let him know that while faith and God were important parts of our lives, we did not want to have a wedding ceremony that focused specifically on Jesus or Allah — simply God. He obliged, including words of faith, prayer, blessings and love in our vows and in his sermon.

We also chose to forgo the traditional religious readings from the Bible or the Quran. We opted instead to have each of our children read a love poem that they had selected for us. This was the perfect way to involve the kids, blend our families and have all of us be together as one for such an extraordinary event.

As is customary in Catholic weddings, we also had a unity candle. This candelabra set includes one large center candle and two smaller candles — one on each side. The side candles signify the individuals in a relationship while the center candle represents their new life together. The symbolism of this piece fit flawlessly into our beliefs that just because we were joining our lives together, we would not lose our identities in the process.

We chose to dress in the traditional American wedding attire. Even thought it was my second marriage, I wore a long white satin dress, accented with lots of sparkling beads. I added a short jacket to cover my shoulders, and a small tiara and veil to match the dress. I wore simple diamond earrings and carried a bouquet of white flowers. Of course, I had a huge smile on my face too! I looked and felt like any anxious and excited bride.

My bridesmaids, Kim and Hassanah, wore long purple satin dresses. They too had short jackets to cover their shoulders, and sparkling silver shoes. They each carried smaller bouquets of purple and white flowers. Being only 14 and 13 at the time, they both looked so beautiful and innocent. Iqbal and Haroon wore traditional black tuxedos with silver and purple vests. Both father and son looked very dapper and handsome.

We had wanted Iqbal's brother, Nasir, to stand up on the groom's side — thus making the bridal party symmetrical. Unfortunately, that's not the way it turned out. Instead the center of attraction was "our new family," as it should have been.

Why didn't Nasir stand up? Well at that time, Iqbal's parents were not speaking to us and the relationship was so strained that we did not want to intensify it more by inviting them to the wedding. We had originally asked Nasir to participate in the festivities, but he called at the last minute telling us that he preferred to "honor thy father and mother" and thus, would not be coming to share in our joy. It would have seemed strange to me to be having such an important event occurring in my life and *not* having my parents or brother there. But it was Iqbal's decision to continue with our lives and our wedding.

So, who did come to our wedding? Well, since this was a second marriage for both of us, we were really in tune with who we wanted to invite. After all, we were paying for this event and could make the rules as we wanted to — not as dictated by mom, dad or whoever held the purse strings.

Our closest friends were — of course — on the top of the invitation list, many of them from Iqbal's work or mine. Next, we invited some of Iqbal's old pharmacy friends and a couple of his cousins. It is interesting to note that Iqbal's cousins did not seem to have the same "disappointment" in his recent life decisions as some other family members. Perhaps it was because they were about the same age or maybe that they just saw how happy Iqbal really was. Since this was a blending of two families, we decided all the spouses and the kids — young and old — should join in our celebration.

The wedding guests also included my family — at least those who could make it. My mom and dad were there along with my brother Dan. Prior commitments and physical distance kept the rest of the family from attending, but they sent their blessings instead.

The reception (immediately following the wedding) was held in the banquet room of the hotel. While we had a harpist play for the actual wedding ceremony, we chose to have a more modern DJ play music while we ate and drank. Dinner was served (salmon and steak, asparagus soup and twice-baked potatoes) and a round of toasts was made for us ... the happy new couple! I should add that non-alcoholic grape juice was provided for anyone (including Iqbal) who was not drinking champagne.

We did have an open bar for anyone who wanted drinks; this too was the result of a compromise. It was new for Iqbal to be at an event — especially a wedding — that served alcohol so freely. I knew he was uncomfortable, but he tried hard not to let it show. No worries were needed however, since our guests kept their senses and did not go too overboard on what and how much was consumed.

Since you can't have a wedding without a cake — we had the traditional cake cutting ceremony shortly after dinner. Our cake, again a blending of both of us, had several layers of white cake with brown mocha frosting in the middle of the layers — note the blending of the brown and white! The decorations on the cake were white with flowers and it was delicious!

Our guests mingled and danced, doing the Macarena and even the limbo. The kids, as much as the adults, were smiling, laughing, and having fun on the dance floor. The photographer snapped pictures — both fun and posed — and everyone had shining smiles on their faces.

We were very happy to have our friends and family with us to share this special day.

The evening ended in a typical wedding way: our guests slowly started to leave and family was all that was left. We had help carrying all the gifts (and some leftover desserts) up to our "honeymoon" suite in the hotel. We said our good-byes and thanked everyone for coming.

Lessons Learned

Enjoy the company of those who celebrate
with you. Don't dwell on those who can't.

Blending yourselves in a marriage doesn't mean you
have to lose your identity, your faith or your beliefs.

CHAPTER 5

Home is Where the Heart Is

After a weeklong honeymoon at the Secrets Excellence Resort in Riviera Maya, Mexico, we came back to *our* house. We had sold Amy's home a few weeks earlier and were settling in to a new life and a new place to live. This was the townhouse I had bought (while it was still under construction) just a few months before Amy and I started dating. I took possession of it in July, but it never dawned on me to ask Amy for her input on everyday things. I just figured that it would all come after we got married. Big mistake!

As soon as I had finished signing the papers, I went out and bought dishes and flatware. To me, these were basic necessities and having them as soon as possible was more important than picking them out with my fiancée. That Friday, I invited Amy over for a home cooked dinner. I was hoping to impress her with my culinary skills and I also wanted to show off our new housewares. She greeted me with a big hug and a smile but after I opened up the cupboards, her mood changed. She barely said a word during dinner and it felt really awkward the rest of the evening. After a few days of not hearing from her, I confronted her about her attitude.

I learned two things in that very moment:

1. *Never* use the word "attitude" when Amy is unhappy, and

2. *Never* buy anything for the house without Amy's input.

What I thought was a sign of responsibility and being compatible, she saw as a sign of male dominance and disrespect. It took us a few days to talk things out and to figure out where we were coming from but in the end, we both agreed that sharing our ideas and the reasons behind them would be better received before taking action.

Over the last few years, Amy and I have decorated and redecorated our home several times. We've taken blank white walls and personalized them into our vision of what a sanctuary should be. From acoustic guitars and prayer rugs to cookbooks and rosary beads, our house reflects our passions, beliefs and similarities. Lucky for us, our tastes in color, style and décor are pretty similar too. We've had some disagreements along the way but Amy and I have learned to compromise on some things and to hold our ground on others. The most obvious one for us was when we began to decorate our house with religious art.

When Amy and Kim moved in, Amy wanted to hang a crucifix in our bedrooms. I knew what the cross was but I didn't know what a crucifix was, so I asked. While most Christians see the cross as a symbol of their faith, Catholics prefer the crucifix (which is a statue of Jesus on the cross). The ones she had in mind were about six inches long and would hang above the entryway of each bedroom. Here was my problem: until that point in my life, I had never had any pictures or statues of people inside my home.

You might be asking yourself, "Why not?" Muslims revere Jesus (Peace Be Upon Him) and his holy mother, Mary, immensely. However, it's forbidden to have pictures or statues of any living creature out of concern that such statues may become the focus of one's worship in place of God Almighty. Without a statue or picture, people won't confuse their focus during daily prayers.

At the same time, I wanted to hang a set of wood-carvings with the name Allah and Muhammad written in Arabic calligraphy. This was something I had grown up with and had used them as visual reminders of my faith. The beautiful designs had always lifted my spirits and helped remind me of my religion. I also needed a dedicated prayer area to pray my five daily prayers facing Mecca. Neither Amy nor I wanted to plaster every room with Catholic and Islamic art, but we also didn't want to feel like we couldn't display them openly in our own home. The common areas of the house needed to reflect both our lives since we shared the house equally.

We decided that the best way to settle the dilemma was to browse for religious décor together. Both of us would share what we liked and didn't like and we agreed to buy only two religious artifacts each. Amy and I agreed to hang her crucifixes above the doors but facing the inside of both bedrooms and we also agreed to hang my wood-cuts on the living room wall near my prayer area. In addition, we also bought several religious plaques that were neither Christian nor Islamic in nature. None mention Allah, Jesus or contain quotes from the Bible or the Quran but continue to inspire us to work good deeds and gain God's grace. My favorite one is, "Pray. You never stand taller than when you are on your knees."

Six months after Amy and I got married, I got a promotion at work! I became a Regional Talent Specialist in the Health & Wellness Division for Wal-Mart and my job required several overnight stays a month. I wasn't going to apply for it at first. After all, I just got married and had a new wife at home. But Amy, knowing my hunger and passion for communicating and connecting with people, assured me that she would be fine.

We promised to call each other every night at 7:00 PM Central Time while I was training and we were pretty good about it too. But sometimes, an event runs longer than expected and when I called Amy two hours later in that last week, I couldn't get past her sobs and tears. She admitted she had been lonely the entire time and had faked being positive to make me feel less worried. She was in desperate need of a furry and cute companion that would love her unconditionally and pay attention to her whenever she walked in the room — much like me!

So began the conversation of bringing home a pet. Like most couples, we discussed who would feed it, clean up after it, wash it, take it for shots, etc. Although we had both owned pets before, I had only owned cats and I was *not* willing to consider a dog.

Don't get me wrong, I like dogs. They're very obedient, loving and wonderful creatures and owning a dog is not forbidden for a Muslim. But, Islam considers a dog's saliva to be impure and since you can never stop a dog from salivating, the chances of having it touch my skin or my clothes was pretty high. Should that happen, my prayers would not be accepted and I would need to take a bath and wash my clothes every single time this happened.

I was also aware of how busy both of us were. Amy woke up every morning at 4:30 AM and didn't get home until 6:30 PM. Who was going to walk the dog when I wasn't home? Lucky for me, Amy had owned a cocker spaniel before and had come to realize (with a little prodding from me) that taking care of a dog is a *ton* more work than having a cute, independent kitten. So, we agreed and two weeks later Amy got Jessie, a calico cat whose purring motor has yet to quit. Both have been happy ever since.

It was around this time that I began to think about my parents and how we had drifted apart. I still lived next door to them but it had been three years since I'd seen or spoken to them. In spite of the fallout, I made sure that Haroon and Hassanah spent several hours every day next door at their Dadi and Dada's. Just because my parents didn't agree with my decision to marry Amy, it wasn't a reason to prevent them from seeing their grandkids or having a relationship with them. No matter how wrong or right I had been, I knew I needed to reconnect with them. The easier of the two would be my mom and I knew the perfect way.

I had become a pretty good cook over the past few years and began to send food next door with the kids. It was a shot in the dark but I figured if I kept it up long enough, they would eventually have to return the containers. A few weeks went by and one night, the kids came home from Dadi/Dada's with samosas — my mom's specialty and my favorite!

The peace treaty was beginning to take shape and we kept sharing food without sending any written messages. It was early summer when I told Haroon and Hassanah to start telling their dadi she was welcome at our house anytime. I expected another six months of exchanging dishes or writing letters back and forth, but to my surprise, she came over the very next week and rang our doorbell! I was shocked and by the grin on her face, and so was Amy!

Here's the weirdest part — my mother and I picked up exactly where we had left off three years prior as if nothing had ever happened! There was no apology, no anger or sadness, no lamenting over lost time. It was as if we just accepted it and moved on. Amy was thrilled and so was my mom. I began to see her weekly, then daily (on days my dad wasn't home). Our relationship had begun to heal, but I was still not ready to speak with my father. They were two very different people and my dad wouldn't be as forgiving. Things would change nine months later.

Mayur (my friend from pharmacy school) had just finished The Landmark Forum and told me that I needed to enroll in it right away. It was a program to help people overcome their own limitations and it was something he strongly recommended. I trusted Mayur implicitly and registered for the class, completely unaware of what to expect. On my very first day, our leader coached me and helped me realize that all the reasons I had used to avoid calling my dad were things I had made up. I hadn't just hurt him by not talking to him, but I had hurt myself for expecting him to apologize to me. It was pure and simple arrogance that I had displayed for four years and it came crashing down that very instant.

I nervously dialed his number and when it went to voicemail, I greeted him with, "Assalam Alaikum" ("may God's peace be on you"), and began to cry uncontrollably. In between the sobs, I apologized for not talking to him and for letting my pride get in the way. I didn't know if he'd call me back but I had taken the first step towards him. To my surprise, he called me the very next day. When I answered the phone, I received a very gruff, "Assalam Alaikum," then began the accusations and angry statements.

I listened quietly and calmly as he vented his frustrations over the next 20 minutes and when it was over, we wished each other well. Despite the nature of this first call, I knew I had opened the door and continued to call him weekly just to pay my respects. As time wore on, I called him more frequently and slowly the signs of distrust and anger began to fade. It took the rest of the year but by February, my parents, Amy and I had finally sat down for our very first meal together.

If you ask our friends and co-workers to describe Amy and me, they'll typically use the words "power-couple." We work 40-plus hours a week, run our own businesses, attend church/masjid regularly and are actively involved in several organizations. Like a lot of couples in our generation, both Amy and I appreciate the importance (and blessing) of both spouses being able to earn a living. Being funny, we both "bring home the bacon," but she's the only one who eats it!

Alternatively, we also understand the need to divide chores around the house. It wouldn't be fair of me to expect Amy to come home after working 14 hours and cook dinner for me. It would be just as unfair if she expected me to be the only one to take out the trash every time. We've come to an agreement on how to divide most household chores in order to keep our home neat and tidy. Amy balances our checkbook, pays the bills and cleans our bathroom. My responsibilities include doing the laundry, vacuuming and loading/unloading the dishwasher.

When it comes to making dinner or going grocery shopping, it's typically something we do together. Sometimes we alternate, depending on who's going out. Like any other couple, sometimes we need reminders but overall it's worked out fine. I can tell you though, that our journey to this understanding was not made overnight.

Before we got married, Amy and I would balance our own checkbooks. My method involved a lot of tenacity (which Amy calls obsessive-compulsive disorder) and I would double check every transaction twice using the paper-method. Amy's technique was much simpler and she used electronic checking to simplify her life! When she began balancing our checkbook, my initial response was not very grown-up. I didn't understand why she wasn't doing it my way — which was obviously better!

I felt that my way had been threatened — not by a woman or a Christian but by someone smarter than me. After several attempts at a discussion, Amy gave me a hug and said that she didn't think my way was wrong, just different ... and more time-consuming. It was at that moment that the light bulb went off and I realized that it had been my mother who did most of the accounting when I was growing up. It took a few hours for me to swallow my pride (again) but I'm glad I gave up my "right to be right" in order to be happy.

Amy had to give up some rights of being right as well to be happy. She had built up a routine to do the laundry every Saturday in a particular way ... between naps! I was more of a "start and get it done" kind of guy. It took her a few months but eventually, Amy understood that if she dropped her need to do the laundry, she'd still have fresh clothes ready for her at the beginning of the work week (courtesy her hubby).

I'd be lying if I said we didn't have issues now and then but none of them ever stem from a religious or cultural reason. We've learned that two reasonable people can easily work things out when we first stop and look at ourselves, recognize our own limitations and accept the hand that's been extended in friendship. It makes things happen so much easier!

Home is Where the Heart Is

✝

Our home is our sanctuary. That's the way it's supposed to be, right? Well, it took us a while to get to that point, but I think we are finally there.

When I first moved in to our house, we had the usual newlywed struggles. Since we had both been married before and had owned homes previously, we had an abundance of furniture, dishes, towels and television sets — literally, we had two households full! So compromise was essential and required — but it wasn't easy.

Iqbal had moved in several months before and had "set up" the house the way he saw fit. This included buying dishes and cookware, arranging the furniture and even putting up a few wall hangings. While I did not immediately object, I didn't feel like it was "my" home, but rather "his" home, in which I was visiting (on a rather permanent basis). Don't get me wrong, it's not that I didn't like what he had brought with him or had recently purchased — it just wasn't mine — or "ours" for that matter. We had not picked anything out together. Now maybe this is just a girl thing, but I needed to be a part of the shopping, arranging, and settling in function that comes with moving into a new house and making it into a home.

I had agreed to sell my furniture and essentially just moved in with my clothes, my shoe collection and a few sentimental items (including my first teddy bear). But as time went by and I tried to settle in, I found that I was missing *my* stuff — *my* couch, *my* chairs, even *my* dog (yes, we decided that having a cocker spaniel was a bit too much to handle in my already busy life). Some days, I wasn't sure whether I was depressed or angry about losing what I thought had been mine.

During that first year, we had a few heated discussions (dare I say arguments?) about what should stay (my teddy bear) and what perhaps we would be better off replacing. We — or should I just say *I* — needed to start fresh and new and *together*!

You might just think that this is no different than any other newly married couple. But unfortunately (with my emotions in over-drive), certain phrases like "Muslim men like to control their wives" kept popping into my head. You might be asking, "What would make you think that?"

Well, one of the questions that I am repeatedly asked when an outsider (i.e., an ill-informed person) finds out that I am married to a Muslim is about gender roles and control issues in our relationship. The stereotyping I had heard (which kept popping into my head) is that in Islam and in the Indian/Pakistani culture, women are to be submissive to the men. Well, I want to go on the record to say that this statement is most definitely *not* true.

During one of our many discussions before we actually got married, Iqbal and I had agreed that everything — and I mean *everything* — was going to be shared 50–50. This meant that neither one of us would control the finances, the household shopping, cooking and cleaning, nor the vacation planning. The only part of our marriage that we would not share in equal parts is how we would raise our children (but more about that later in the book).

Over the course of the next few years, we slowly began to replace some of his old things (bed, couches and drapes) and pick out our own beautiful style of home furnishings. Not only did we have fun browsing together and imagining our house with a new trinket, but we kept each other from going "overboard" on any one crazy idea. For example, he once thought about putting a canopy and sheer draping all around our bed!

When it comes to religious decorations (not including the seasonal Christmas tree), we have agreed to share the space in our house and limit our pictures, statues, etc. to a modest amount. We each have our favorite pieces, many of which we either collected or received as gifts over the years. These things, mostly wall art, are displayed throughout the house.

Contrary to popular belief, we do not have a Muslim section and a Catholic section in the house or even in any one room. Instead, just as Iqbal and I live together in harmony, so do our religious adornments. In truth, many of our chosen pieces are really non-denominational, simply praising God or saying a prayer. One item, however, that I would not compromise on is a small plaque that says, "The Jesus in Me Loves You." My parents gave me that sign for my first communion when I was in the second grade and it has been hanging on the wall next to my bed ever since.

I never would have thought that my husband's religion would make a difference in what particular art I chose to display in my home. Coming from a modest Catholic upbringing, I wasn't about to have any wild pictures of naked people or such. But what I found out while shopping one day was much more basic. Muslims are not supposed to have any pictures or sculptures of people — especially with their faces showing. As I had begun to expect, everything about my relationship would be a learning experience!

Muslims believe that keeping pictures and statues in a room of prayer prevents angels from coming into that room or house and may not "record" the prayer being performed. In addition, keeping pictures and statues of any being (human or creature) is a slippery slope towards idol worship and thus these things are encouraged not to be kept in the house. Regardless of decorating preferences, if you were to walk into our home, I would hope that you feel the warmth and love that exists inside.

Now back to those chores for a minute. How do we break them up? As far as I can tell, we do it the same way every other family does (or should!). A certain "division of labor," so to speak, is necessary in order to get the chores done and have a happy and loving household. Since both Iqbal and I work outside the home (well, kind of — I'll explain in a minute) and the kids are teenagers, we divided all the chores. Luckily, Iqbal gets to work out of the house on days he is not traveling so he graciously agreed to do our laundry (the kids do their own) as well as feed the cat, take out the garbage, vacuum and do the majority of the cooking. I, on the other hand, handle the financial matters, do the shopping — both grocery and retail — dust and clean the bathrooms (which recently includes the cat's as well).

Now that's not to say that we each don't have our own little quirks. The bed must be made (usually by Iqbal), the living room coffee table and the kitchen table are sometimes scattered with papers (both of ours) and there are cat toys everywhere (the cat is to blame for this one)! If we have company coming over, we both chip in to get the whole house cleaned up and looking sharp.

As for the cooking, Iqbal does the majority. Lately, he has been experimenting with various spices, meats and vegetables to come up with some tasty and aromatic dishes. Every week or so, he will look up a new recipe, use Zabiha meat (beef or chicken that has been Islamically blessed upon slaughtering) and invite his parents to share in the creation. We have found some wonderful new favorites — and a few that we will never make again!

I get my turn in the kitchen too. Since repairing our relationship with Iqbal's parents, I have had the opportunity to learn first-hand how to make some very delicious Indian dishes. When time permits, I will whip up some of my traditional dishes, including pastas, desserts and potatoes — any kind! Remember, I'm Irish!

When it comes to our clothes, I will admit that religion does play a role. Being raised Catholic, I was taught that my clothing should be conservative, not too revealing. When I wear a dress, it generally stops right at knee length and if I happen to wear a tank top or cami, I always have a sweater on over it when I leave the house. My shorts are mid-thigh length (the typical middle-aged woman's), although lately I've found myself wearing capris more than shorts. I don't know if this is really due to any faith or cultural perspectives being cast on to me from Iqbal or just my own middle-aged woman preference.

I do, however, take an extra minute or two to consider what I am wearing when we go to see my in-laws or over to one of Iqbal's relative's homes. While I don't consider my shirts to be too low cut, I do make sure that they are not too fitted or show too much skin.

I own a few shalwar kameez (Indian dress for women, often referred to as "suits") and I do like wearing them to Indian parties or on special occasions (such as Eid). Iqbal and his mom helped me buy my first few and Iqbal's mom has given me some as gifts as well. These outfits — mostly silk adorned with embroidery and jewels — are always paired with the traditional large Indian costume jewelry (the almost shoulder length dangling earrings, matching necklaces and bangle bracelets). I must say they are very ornate and comfortable as well.

Another particularly interesting thing about the suits is that it is perfectly acceptable to wear patterns and colors that make you happy. There do not seem to be the "seasonal" color or style issues that there are with traditional western clothes. If you like pink, wear pink! And the color combinations on some of the outfits are definitely nothing that I would have thought to put together (although when it's a complete outfit, it looks terrific).

In the privacy of our own home, however, you can usually find me in my work clothes — typically slacks and a top or a pantsuit on weekdays and pajama pants or jeans on evenings and weekends. For special dinners (with just Iqbal or friends), I usually wear a dress or slacks and a sweater. While many Indian women may choose to wear a cotton shalwar kameez at home, I'm quite happy in my western attire.

I do own and wear a swimsuit, of course only when I am going swimming. Having grown up around a swimming pool, I am still quite comfortable wearing my racing suit — whether it be to the health club to work out or to the resort pool when we are on vacation. Ever since my early twenties, I have had a one-piece suit, which I believe is Iqbal's preference anyway. When I have mentioned getting anything else, he squirms but does not comment. I can feel his reluctance to dictate my choices but I can tell he is definitely sensitive to a woman (especially his wife) showing too much skin. No worries, honey — at my age, a two-piece swimsuit is out of the question!

Iqbal has a few Kortas, or Indian men's dress shirts, too. Like me, he saves these to wear on special occasions. He typically dresses up in a suit and tie for a formal affair or slacks and a blazer for a more casual event. Most other days you can find him in jeans and a T-shirt, or perhaps a long sleeve cotton shirt.

Lastly, one other important difference you may find in our home is that we take off our shoes when we enter the house. We request that visitors do the same. This had been a rule in my old house for many years, mostly just to save on the wear and tear (and tracking of mud) on the carpet. I didn't realize it though (until I married Iqbal) that it also now serves another purpose — it keeps the house clean, which is needed for him to pray. For completely different reasons, we are both very happy with this practice!

I don't typically think of our home, our daily routine and our habits as being related at all to faith or culture. However, when I stop to think about it, perhaps it always has been. The similarities between Islam and Catholicism (at least in this aspect) are so close, you might never notice the difference.

Lessons Learned

Sharing is important in both love
and household chores.

Different ways of doing things isn't
wrong, it's just different.

Loving involves giving up the right to always be right.

CHAPTER 6

Eat, Drink, and Be Merry

Amy and I are both foodies. If you're not familiar with what I just called myself, a "foodie" is someone who has a deep, passionate interest in food. We love the aroma of food, the color of food, the presentation, history and culture behind our food. I'm more of a traditionalist and Amy is more about experimenting and creating brand new (and strange) concoctions. But together, we are one mean "foodie" couple!

Ever since our first date at Giordano's, Amy and I have discovered an intense pleasure in visiting different restaurants that serve all kinds of different cuisines. We compare the quality of menu items, discuss entrées with the head chef and learn something new about our food every chance we get.

Food plays a key role in building strong relationships between people across all faiths and cultures. I'm sure you've heard (or even used) the term "breaking bread" before. It comes from the Last Supper and shines a light on the brotherhood between Jesus (pbuh) and his 12 Disciples. Sharing a meal together creates love, friendship and a deep sense of trust. It's something Amy, the kids and I did and we shared a lot of laughs and learned about each other in the process. Most importantly, it fostered a sense of family, and even though my son is in college now, we still have him over at least once a week to share a meal.

The opposite is just as true. When one is invited but declines to eat with another, it can easily be taken as a sign of disrespect. In Eastern and Middle Eastern cultures, it's considered a serious insult. When I was growing up, it was impossible to go to over a relative's house and not eat. "Don't be rude" my mother would say, but she obviously didn't see the connection between our visits with Munnee Aapa (my aunt) and me wearing "husky-size" jeans. Blending both East and West at home was a challenge, but it was also an opportunity to share our beliefs and backgrounds.

Early on, Amy and I had talked about what my kids and I could eat and what we wouldn't. The biggest issue for us was to avoid pork. As Muslims, it's forbidden for us to eat the meat from a pig or foods containing pork because they are considered unclean. There's plenty of literature out there about the harmful effects pork has on the human body and if you're interested, you can find it all online. Orthodox Jews follow the same law and the early Christians did as well. Amy had grown up eating everything and wasn't about to change — and I didn't want her to either. I just wanted her to help me and my kids be good Muslims.

Growing up, my family spent a lot of time in grocery aisles researching meats and packaged goods to see if it was ok to buy or if it stayed on the shelf. Some products are pretty obvious to identify like sausage, ham, Spam, pepperoni, hot dogs, bratwurst, bacon, ribs and pork chops. Those are definite no-nos and we avoid them like the plague, but there are others that you just can't tell at first glance.

On a recent to trip to Italy, Amy and I had ordered spaghetti with meat sauce, thinking it was ground beef. As the plate arrived, it looked kind of like beef and kind of not. I asked the waiter what was the "meat" in meat sauce and in a beautiful, thick Italian accent he replied, "Pork and beef!" I stuck to cheese pizza the rest of the trip.

Anyhow, my request didn't faze Amy a bit and she was totally committed to helping me stick to the plan. But when I told her that we would need to be very careful about sharing spoons, forks and other utensils in the kitchen as well as at the dinner table, her left eyebrow went up.

"Why?" she asked and I explained to her that that if it had been in contact with anything containing pork, my kids and I couldn't use it. That meant either washing it again with soap and hot water or using a brand new one. It sounds simple but when you're cooking for five and one dish is pork and beans, it's almost guaranteed you'll use the same spoon to stir another pot. "Parenting" took on a whole new meaning for us after that.

When the kids were younger, we'd have movie marathons during their winter breaks. But none of them shared our foodieness back then and Amy and I typically lost the "what's for dinner?" battle and ordered pizza. We always made sure to order two: one pepperoni and one plain cheese. If we needed to use the pizza cutter, we always cut the cheese one first to avoid "contamination" from that "icky" pepperoni one. Sharing chips and cookies with each other was pretty common in our house, but Amy and I were always on the lookout for something that might go unnoticed. For a while, we called each other "FGs" — the "Food Gestapo" — and it took some time for Amy to get used to it.

Although we both shop for groceries, Amy likes to spend half a day doing it. I love her but I've also learned that time is in short supply. So I typically tend to let her have her fun shopping while I play catch-up at the office or go for a bike ride. According to *The Five Love Languages*, by Dr. Gary Chapman, Amy's primary language is "Receiving Gifts." Telling her "I love you" is nice but giving her a gift (especially something sparkly and expensive) puts her on Cloud Nine! She shows love the same way and always picks up a few "goodies" for each of us to share. Knowing our restrictions, Amy's been pretty good about not bringing home a honey-baked ham for dinner, but we hadn't discussed pork by-products. A pork by-product is an ingredient that contains pork in any way, shape or form. You can find them listed as lard, animal shortening (pork) and gelatin.

Amy knows I have a sweet tooth (particularly for cookies) but the ones she bought for me typically had animal shortening (pork). So you can imagine her frustration and disappointment when I said, "No, thank you." I had just taken her gift and returned it, essentially telling her (in her language), "I *don't* love you." It was a learning experience to say the least, but we kept working at it.

In fact, we replayed this scenario several times over the next few months when she'd buy me cookies, pie crusts, corn and potato chips, chip dip, snack bars, and marshmallows. Over the years, Amy has learned (mostly through trial and error) to examine the list of ingredients with a magnifying glass a couple of times before dropping it into the cart. It's out of love that she buys me things and now, out of respect for my faith, she's become pretty good at spotting the culprits.

This hasn't deterred Amy and Kim from eating bacon, ham or anything else that once went "oink." In fact, bacon is a staple of my step-daughter's diet and there's yet to be a day where she has gone without. To this disgusting — uh ... *amazing* — feat, all I have to say is "teenagers!" We've all learned to clearly label "pork chops" on Ziploc bags before tossing them into the freezer. We make sure that sliced ham is in a tightly-sealed container with a special colored lid before placing it in the fridge next to the shaved turkey breast.

When Amy has a craving for a Hawaiian pizza (pineapple, ham and cheese), she'll order it when I'm out of town and devour it in one night. There is a drawback to all of this though — I won't kiss Amy on the lips when she eats pork. Because the juices from the meat can transfer from mouth to mouth, I won't lock lips and we won't share spoons and forks. Lucky for me, she's pretty good about eating the stuff when I'm not around or when she's at work. After a few hours have passed and she has snacked on other things, I'll still greet her with a kiss when she comes home!

Amy and I have become wiser over the years and have learned to ask specific questions of our waiter. We both love steak and when we're out on a date, we'll share different cuts with each other. It's not the steak that we find issues with, but the sides that come with it. We've discovered (sometimes a little too late) that certain restaurants add bacon or ham to their baked potatoes, soups, salads, and pastas without being asked. There is no mention of it on the menu.

A few months ago, Amy and I had dinner at a well-known chain Italian restaurant. We had both read the menu very carefully before

I ordered the cheese-stuffed pasta with beef medallions. It all looked fine and tasted pretty good, until I discovered that the tiny red bits in the sauce were pieces of ham! I had asked the waitress before ordering and she had clearly said that there was no pork. The manager profusely apologized and agreed that the company should have clearly listed it on their menu. Even though the restaurant gave us a full refund, the damage had been done.

Alcohol was the other big thing Amy and I didn't see eye-to-eye on. Islam considers drinking alcohol a major sin because it causes people to lose control and clouds their judgment. It's been said that a Muslim who produces, carries, serves, transports, sells, buys or drinks alcohol commits the same sin. It's pretty serious stuff. On the contrary, the Christian faith not only allows its consumption, but Catholics drink wine as part of their holy communion as a symbol of Christ's blood.

Not all Christians drink, but those that do cite how Jesus turned water into wine, which they find makes them feel more comfortable. Amy jokes that for an Irish-Polish Catholic *not* to drink would be a sin! It wasn't an issue for us when we were just dating. She'd never drink in front of me and we both went back to our own home at the end of the night.

The first time Amy "openly" had a drink was when we went to see a Cirque Du Soleil show. It was a hot day and she was dying of thirst, so we went to the bar. I had expected her to order some lemonade or a bottle of water but instead, she asked for a strawberry daiquiri! Now I knew she drank beer and she *really* loved vodka. For years, I'd watched her party with the guys at our annual Tae Kwon Do Christmas party and she jokingly admitted she was a "lush." Amy definitely knew how to throw back a few and even some of the guys admitted defeat when going head-to-head in a drinking game.

But this time, it was different. We weren't just friends, we were a couple! Having seen so many people get plastered at a party, I knew my discomfort level would rise and I would leave. It had happened year after year and I didn't like being around people who "turned ugly." Even worse, we were on a date! I wasn't going to leave Amy but I didn't want to see her get out of control.

Leave it to Amy's investigative skills, but she picked up on my awkward silence almost immediately. She looked at me, looked at her drink, and asked, "Are you uncomfortable with me drinking?" "Yes!" I replied (rather quickly) and started rambling on about my concerns, the potential mistakes she might make being intoxicated, the ramifications of her making a scene, and possibly being arrested! Yeah, I was on a roll. She smiled, touched my arm and explained (calmly I might add) that she would not get drunk in front of me, especially after one sip. She just missed the taste and was confident one drink wouldn't put her over the edge. I trusted her and even though it took me a few hours to get over my self-induced anxiety, I eventually did.

We did a lot of give and take after getting married, especially when we were putting Amy's house on the market. One evening, I was helping Amy clean up her home and took the liberty of putting all of her wine and alcohol in a box and threw them in the dumpster. She was more confused than mad about why I was making such a big deal about this one thing. It was hard to explain, but just being around alcohol made me uncomfortable. It took us a couple of years for Amy and me to get a handle on this, but we finally did.

Amy drinks occasionally and when she does, it's only a glass or two at the most. She's cut down for me, but it's also because she's been trying to eat healthy as well. She'll have an occasional glass of Pinot Grigio or a French martini if we're out on a date, but I've gotten used to it. We don't keep beer in the house, but Amy does keep a bottle of wine for those nights she's in the mood for a glass. I've come to understand that Amy really does know her limits and she's not looking to get smashed. I've also realized that pushing my views about alcohol isn't fair and it's not going to stop her from drinking. Forcing someone to conform to your view wasn't what we had set out to do and with a lot of patience and reminding from Amy, I finally got the picture.

Eat, Drink, and Be Merry

✝

"Is this pork?" I can honestly say I've been asked that question at least 100 times since I've been married to Iqbal — and each time by him! As I'm sure you know, Muslims do not eat pork or anything made from it. That means no bacon, no ham and no baby back ribs, but it also means no Jell-O, no marshmallows and sometimes no gravy or sauces.

Quite frequently, I am asked about the dynamics of our daily life, especially when it comes to food. It seems that some people believe that Iqbal (and therefore I) can *only* eat Indian food. I'll admit before I married Iqbal, I don't think I really had authentic Indian cuisine, but certainly that is not the only type of food we eat.

Like any couple, we have our favorite dishes that we enjoy making and sharing with each other. Of course, there are those that we still eat even if the other person doesn't like it. For me, this can be summed up in two items — bacon and Hawaiian pizza! If Iqbal wants to ensure an evening alone, all he needs to do is break open a bag of Doritos — I can't stand the smell!

One of my favorite ways to spend a Sunday is to lazily roll out of bed, put on a pot of coffee and cook up two eggs (over-easy) and a few strips of bacon. To top it off, I'll butter up a slice of whole wheat toast. If I feel like making it extra special, I'll even add half a grapefruit for a full breakfast feast. Now I don't get to spoil myself every day — or even every weekend for that matter — but it is a treat I can enjoy, just not with Iqbal.

Iqbal and I will try to find the perfect balance between our tastes or cheerfully give in if one of us has a particular craving for something special. I would have to say though, that 99 percent of the meals I now cook are made with no pork or pork products. This means that sometimes I have to modify the recipe, exchanging turkey for ham or perhaps spinach for bacon. When we are at home, this is usually pretty easy. After all, we *know* what we are putting in the pan and therefore into our mouths.

I must confess that when Iqbal is in town, he does the majority of the cooking. He loves to cook and since he works at home (when he's not traveling), it just seems to satisfy us both. He's a great cook and I'm certainly not going to complain!

When we decide to eat a meal out, however, we have a different arrangement. Iqbal will order food that doesn't have pork and 99 percent of the time, I will too. We like to share our food — swapping half a sandwich or salad with each other. Since we enjoy doing this (it adds variety to every meal), I am conscious of what I order and try to get foods that Iqbal can eat as well. On occasion, we are surprised at what is served and have found that it is sometimes easier to have me sample the food to ensure that is in fact beef and not pork. This is especially true when it comes to meatballs, certain pasta dishes and even some sauces. Although you might think that it's easy to just look on the menu to see if the item contains bacon or ham, we have been surprised to find that many restaurants cook with bacon. Apparently (since it is not a main ingredient), they don't feel the need to list it. Lately if we have a question, we have learned to check with the chef just to be sure and then we can sit back, relax, and enjoy a worry-free dinner.

Some restaurants can be even more of an adventure then we thought. As you might expect, Iqbal and I will pick restaurants that have a variety of items that he can choose from. Most of the time, we find we are quite satisfied with the selections offered. It seems that more and more restaurants are at least offering seafood or vegetarian options and that makes it easier for non-pork eaters. But one night, we had a really bad experience.

About two years into our marriage, we decided to patronize restaurants that we had never been to before. We had been in a rut of only going to the same three or four places over and over and over again so we decided it would be a year to try new things.

As we drove down "restaurant row," we selected a place that served German food. Since neither of us had been there, we figured we'd be in for an exciting time trying out some new tasty dishes. Unfortunately, our own naïveté caught up with us and what we found both surprised and shocked us. Everything — I swear everything — was cooked in lard or contained bacon or ham of some variety. Although we had looked at the menu before ordering and did the best job we could, when the food arrived, we both took one look at each other and shook our heads. I was going to have a *lot* to eat that night and Iqbal was going to go hungry. There didn't seem to be even one appetizer or entrée that was suitable for Iqbal! Obviously, we haven't gone back to that restaurant since.

You should know that from a social perspective, sharing food with my husband — whether it's lunch, dinner or just a snack — hits the top of my list. It's our time together to talk, share our day and share in the wonderful flavors and sensations of various cuisines. When we first were married, I thought to myself, "It's okay if he doesn't eat pork. No problem, he just won't eat pork." But to be honest, my new found "restrictions" (due to Iqbal's religious practice) have made it difficult at times for me to make, eat and share some of the foods I love. This is especially true of my traditional religious holiday favorites — an Easter ham or a Christmas Eve pork roast.

In the past five years though, I have come to find a balance with this "pork issue." When Iqbal and I are together, I am very conscious of what I order and eat — Iqbal won't even give me a kiss if I've recently eaten bacon! But when he is out of town, I pull out all the stops and order a Hawaiian pizza (Canadian bacon and pineapple) or make pork chops. When I'm down in the city for work, I can eat generally anything I want (the health side of this remark is a whole different story).

While we seem to have found the right compromises when it comes to the food restrictions, that's not all that an intercultural relationship is about. Next come the ethnic cuisine and manners.

Recently, we have been getting together with Iqbal's parents for Sunday brunch. I will usually make some sweets or muffins to take along and Iqbal may make a new dish he is trying out. Zulekha almost always has seasoned eggs, as well as Nihari or keema (ground beef) with potatoes. Huh! Now that I stop and think about it, it's interesting that all of Zulekha's food is spicy and my traditional Midwestern fare is on the bland side. Anyway, we typically also have paratha (tortilla type bread) along with the meal. Since the menu doesn't change much from visit to visit, I've come to expect these foods and look forward to our gatherings — but that was not always the case.

My first experience eating with Iqbal's family I remember being a bit "uneasy." We sat down at the table, me sitting next to Iqbal and taking my cues on etiquette from him. The food was served buffet style, since most of it was hot and freshly made waiting for us on the stove. I got my plate, took a small spoonful of each item and returned to my seat. When everyone sat down, I was ready to eat. That's when I noticed there was no silverware at my place or at anyone else's! At first, I just stopped and stared. Then I realized, no one was using a fork or a spoon either. Instead, they used the paratha to scoop up the eggs, meat and vegetables — and then just ate with their fingers! Although this was new for me, I wasn't one to fight an adventure, so I joined in, learning the art of tearing the chicken into bite size pieces and not being worried (or bothered) with getting sauce on my hands.

After brunch came my favorite part of the meal — chai or tea. We Americans call it "chai tea," which literally translated would mean, "tea tea" — how little we know! While it's a tradition in many Indian cultures, it is also very common in Great Britain. My mother-in-law makes hers with black tea, evaporated milk and a bit of cardamom. It is delicious and honestly the best I've ever had! It is the perfect way to end the meal.

Iqbal and I have been experimenting as of late with new recipes that we've found in books, magazines and even from restaurants. We've cooked up quite a variety of dishes of all types of cuisines and shared many with his parents. They only eat Zabiha meat so sometimes, we don't always share. His mother will do the same when she is cooking, so we are never short on either the quantity or the variety of what we put on the table. I have taken up the habit as well — even attempting to cook some Indian dishes (especially the traditional ones that Zulekha makes), although I don't quite have those spices down yet!

I'll admit though, that I still love to go out to eat. Some types of food are just best left to those chefs that specialize in it. My favorite restaurant meal is a good old ribeye steak and baked potato. Living in Chicago, I have my choice of amazing places to pick from and what better way to complete a great steak dinner than a glass of wine. Well, for me at least!

As a rule, Muslims do not drink alcohol or serve it or have it in the house. I believe when we first got married, Iqbal would have appreciated it if I had followed along. But being who I am (and dare I tease because I'm both Irish and Polish), I enjoy a nice cocktail or glass of wine every now and then.

Before Iqbal and I were married, I used to have my "liquor" cabinet that had all the fixings for my favorite drinks — daiquiris, screwdrivers, and cosmopolitans as well as an ample supply of white Zinfandel and light beer. After a long day at work or a hot summer day, a nice cool glass of wine or bottle of beer would hit the spot!

But when I started dating Iqbal (especially when we were first married), my fondness for alcohol caused a few less than pleasant discussions. Iqbal was definitely not used to having any alcohol in the house — and of course I was on the opposite end of the spectrum (not used to having *no* alcohol in the house)! It wasn't that I was drinking every day or that I even wanted to drink every day. I believed that for Iqbal, it was just the fact that it was in the house. From my perspective, his dislike of this was more of a stab at my rights and equality in a marriage. In my mind, I wasn't forcing him to drink and it was my house too, so why couldn't I have what I wanted in the cabinet or the fridge?

Well, after a few episodes of having all the beer poured down the drain and a few more heated discussions, we finally came to some understanding. Iqbal acquiesced to the thought of having a bottle of wine chilling in the fridge and I agreed that I didn't really need to keep a supply of beer on hand — especially now that I was no longer in college. Although it still does seem to bother Iqbal on occasion — especially the smell of the beer — I do enjoy a glass of Pinot Grigio now and then, but typically save my beer drinking for a night out with friends.

Lessons Learned

☪ ✝

Be patient while you learn to live with others.

Don't abandon your position just to please someone else. Find ways to work together.

Help your friends stay true to their beliefs.

CHAPTER 7

Celebrating the Holidays

Amy and I like to share. We've found common ground on a lot of different issues because of it. It's as if we have an unspoken motto: the more you share, the more you care! In fact, one of the very best things we've gotten to share with each other is our holidays.

We've gone from celebrating two holidays each to celebrating five (not counting birthdays and anniversaries). What's even better is that we share them with our families — something that seemed impossible not too long ago. My family and I celebrate two big holidays together: Eid-ul-Adha and Eid-ul-Fitr. Eid-ul-Adha commemorates the sacrifice of Ismail (not Isaac according to our beliefs) by Prophet Abraham (p.b.u.h) and Eid-ul-Fitr commemorates the end of Ramadan — our month of fasting.

On both occasions, my family and I dress up and go to masjid for a special morning prayer and then we invite our friends and family from all over Chicago to celebrate with us. It's a huge party and as a special reward for fasting, all the little boys and girls get envelopes full of cash from their aunts and uncles. Like most holidays around the world, there are some standard dishes that make both Eids complete: Nihari (a delicious spicy beef dish that's the national dish of Pakistan) and Suna

Mukhi Halwa (a traditional Burmese sweet dish made with coconut milk, sugar and semolina).

About the only thing that's changed since Amy and I got married is that Amy (being the new girl in the family) goes shopping every year with my mom and gets a very special (and expensive) Eid present: new Indian clothes and jewelry. Aside from that, it's difficult to distinguish the differences between my family and Amy's. The hours we spend together eating, talking politics (men) or comparing pretty dresses and jewelry (women), talking about each other's spouses ... yeah, pretty much the same in both families and across most cultures as well.

Christmas had an entirely different meaning for me than Amy when I was growing up. They call it "Winter Break" now to be politically correct, but even as a kid, my brother and I knew that the two weeks we got off from school was a special time for everyone regardless of faith or nationality. It was special to me because I got to watch a *ton* of Christmas specials! *Frosty the Snowman, Rudolph the Red-Nosed Reindeer* and *The Year Without a Santa Claus* became the cornerstone of my childhood memories. They were constant reminders that (at least during Christmas), people needed to be friendlier and more generous than they usually were — especially when dealing with a Mr. Heat Miser or Mr. Snow Miser of their own!

Besides the hours of claymation and cartoons, we didn't celebrate Christmas at all. There were no presents to exchange, no tree to decorate and no Christmas dinner. It just wasn't our holiday. In fact, my brother laughed at me one year when I told him one day that Santa was going to visit us. Year after year, my parents and grandparents would remind me that these holidays weren't ours and that we had our own Islamic holidays.

The one exception to all this was the annual drive my dad took my mom, my brother and me on through Lincolnwood to see all the fancy Christmas decorations. In retrospect, it seemed weird that that we didn't put up our own decorations but were eager enough to brave the ice and snow to catch a glimpse of them on other people's lawns. We would drive past the richest homes in Chicago to see the biggest, brightest and most colorful displays around. I carried on this tradition with my kids when they were younger but stopped a few years ago.

Before we got engaged, Amy and I had started to talk more openly about our different faiths and practices. We were working towards understanding each other better and secretly, I think we were both looking for some insight into what *our* future might look like.

One particular night, we decided to play "make-believe," and Amy asked me to describe how I saw our life as husband and wife. Now, I'm not very good at imagining things and to this day, Amy balances her laughter and frustration with me when she accuses me of being too literal. When I told her I had a "creative deficiency," she took the lead and described the many Christmases she had growing up, the traditions she started with her daughter and how she pictured us spending Christmas together by the tree. She must have noticed a blank look on my face and after a slight pause, Amy asked me to try again. Not having had any experiences of my own in decorating a tree or hanging stockings, I simply replied, "I don't know." The conversation stopped very abruptly and since it was getting late, we decided I should go home.

The very next morning, I received a very lengthy email with the subject line "Trees, Beer and Marriage" from a very, very unhappy Amy. Something had gotten lost in translation and she couldn't understand why I wasn't willing to even consider allowing her to celebrate Christmas if we got married. My best guess was that she had misconstrued my "I don't know" to mean "No, we will not have a tree in *my* house!" After leaving her ten voicemails with no reply, I drove over with a dozen roses in the hopes that she would open the door. The flowers worked and when Amy finally opened the door, I gave her a long hug and explained to her that I couldn't just make up something about Christmas if I hadn't ever experienced it. It wasn't the way my mind worked.

Amy and I talked a lot that night and we came to realize that both of us had certain expectations for a second marriage. As much as we loved each other, neither of us would entertain the idea of converting. It was also true that neither of us expected the other to convert either. When it came to the holidays, I was willing to experience all the fun and festivities of a Christmas and Easter and she was willing to experience the joys and pleasure of Eid-ul-Adha and Eid-ul-Fitr. It was probably our first "compromise" but we were aware of how much more we'd get out of this deal than we'd give up.

Our first Christmas together reminded me of every TV family sit-com's Christmas special. The snow had been falling for weeks and our radio had been tuned to the all-Christmas-music station since December 1. All three kids, Amy and I put up the tree and decorated it with sparkling new ornaments. On Christmas Eve, we celebrated our first Christmas dinner and afterwards, we sat in front of the fireplace laughing and playing board games. We woke up the next morning to the love-fest of presents. It lasted 2 hours as Amy — um, I mean Santa — had left 15 presents for each of us to help celebrate our first Atcha Christmas.

While Christmas has become the annual tradition Amy had dreamed it would be, it's brought some other welcome changes as well. After years of ignoring each other, my parents and I buried the hatchet and last year, they graciously accepted our invitation to come over for Christmas dinner. It felt a little strange at first to exchange gifts with my parents, but Amy's charisma and gift-giving spirit erased any awkward-ness in minutes.

This year, we weren't able to invite them over because we experi-enced another first. Amy, Kim and I flew to Houston, Texas, to celebrate the first full Arcy Christmas in 20-plus years! Her entire family (mother, father, step-mother, brothers and their families) flew or drove in and we spent an entire week at her brother Dan's and sister-in-law Debbie's house. Between playing with my five-month-old nephew and niece, taking Eddie (the dog) for a walk, and spending time with the entire family, it was also a prime opportunity to create a new tradition: the Annual Arcy Cook-off!

Known for their culinary skills, the three siblings prepared and served three dishes to the entire family but the best part was that *we* were the judges! It was a lot of fun and although Matt (the youngest brother) went home with the trophy, Amy and Dan are more determined than ever to get it back from him next year!

My first Easter experience came while we were still dating. It was a weekend I didn't have the kids and Amy had invited me to spend Easter with her and Kim. When I arrived, she handed me a basket of chocolate and sat me down. I looked at the basket, looked at Kim (who was smiling ear to ear) and looked at Amy. "What the heck is this?" I said to myself. I knew all about the Easter bunny and that Christians celebrated Jesus's resurrection but ... why did I get a basket?

Amy has a child-like spirit and loves to make people feel young. It's one of the things that make me love her so very much! She had decorated and hidden two dozen Easter eggs throughout her house and it was up to Kim and me to find them all! Not really having a choice, I smiled and set out to find them but wouldn't you know it, Kim found all but three? Gee.

Amy still loves to hide Easter eggs and until just last year, she and all three kids would sit down at the table coloring and decorating for hours on end. The first year after we got married, my kids were all about the Easter Egg Hunt and Haroon set to finding all the eggs like a hound on a fox's trail! It was a great memory and Amy still gets them an Easter basket filled with *tons* and *tons* of chocolate.

Easter dinners have also become a tradition: Cornish hens with long-grain wild rice. The nutty-buttery flavor of the rice combined with the small, and meaty hens are actually pretty good. Still, they don't compare to the Reese's Peanut Butter Eggs I get in my basket every year!

Celebrating Christian holidays as a Muslim has been pretty amazing for me. Amy feels the same way when she talks about our Muslim holidays. Her family knows I'm Muslim and my family knows Amy is Catholic. Still, what amazes us both is how comfortable they are in sharing their faith and culture with us. We see their willingness to actively involve us in their traditions as a sign of love and acceptance.

It's clear to us how our respective Muslim and Christian holidays may never have been introduced to the other Atchas and Arcys without Amy or me. But after years of living in Chicago, what I couldn't understand was why my family hadn't embraced Thanksgiving — the most secular and American of holidays. Maybe they always saw it as "American" and weren't interested in losing their own identity. Whatever the reason, it wasn't until Amy and I got married that we made it a tradition in the Atcha household.

I've always seen Thanksgiving as the one and only holiday where family comes first. No cards, no gifts, no shopping for presents of any kind, just food and the spirit of togetherness. I had celebrated Thanksgiving for many years with Haroon and Hassanah's other grandparents, so I wasn't a stranger to the tradition at all. Amy and I invited Naveed (my close friend and financial planner) to our first Thanksgiving together and we woke up at 6:00 AM to pop the bird in the oven. With the kids' help, we made the gravy, mashed potatoes, crescent rolls and green bean casserole. Haroon made pumpkin spice bread and Naveed brought French silk pie. After a very filling Thanksgiving meal, the boys challenged the girls to play the board game Pictionary and thus, a new tradition was born.

We enjoyed our new tradition so much, we had Thanksgiving with Naveed again the following year and this time, we even invited my mother-in-law! Of course, the word got around and Amy's family wanted in on the action too. Actually, they had this tradition way before we did and were inviting us to Bastrop, Texas for Thanksgiving with her dad and brother, Dan. It reminded me a lot of Eid where we spent hours together eating, talking politics (men) and comparing pretty dresses and jewelry (women), talking about each other's spouses ... yup, exactly the same.

After two years of flying to Texas, we decided to take a break this year and invited my mother-in-law and my parents to resume our tradition. The kids were at their other parents' houses and it was an all adults Thanksgiving. It was a wonderful time nevertheless and the most miraculous thing happened! I've made it a habit to say grace (using

Islamic prayers) and to give thanks to God before every meal. Amy and I always hold hands as we say our own words before we eat and invite others to join us. It's not a typical Muslim thing, but it's not wrong to do it either. As Amy and I held hands, my mother-in-law, my mother and my father joined us and we said both a Catholic and Islamic grace out loud. Amen/Ameen!

Celebrating the Holidays

✝

As with most families, Iqbal and I have parties at our house and at other relatives' too. There is always something exciting about getting together with friends — whether it be for a holiday, a birthday, a special occasion or just an ordinary weekend that turns into something more.

Our first party together was right after Iqbal and I got engaged. One sunny Saturday afternoon in the late summer, we invited two of Iqbal's cousins over to his house along with their wives. These cousins, Adnan and Irfan, were more than just relatives to Iqbal — they had been childhood friends. The three "boys" had grown up together in Chicago and were very close. This was my first interaction with his "family" and honestly, I was nervous.

We decided to have a cookout with the usual hamburgers, grilled chicken and a few side dishes. We all ate, sat and talked and afterwards I thought, "Well, that went just fine. I wonder why I was so nervous."

These cousins are about the same age as Iqbal and although both are married to Muslim women, they are of the same generation and seemed to be fine with me — "the white woman." I believe that they were just glad that Iqbal was happy.

It was a typical cookout as far as I was concerned but without the alcohol. We did dress a little bit fancier than I was used to (no jeans, khaki pants instead), but still western-style clothing. Other than those two things, the gathering was nothing out of the ordinary. Although I had never met his cousins or their wives before, they graciously welcomed me into their family with hugs and smiles. Little did I know at the time that future events would be much different.

The next party we hosted was in December 2010. This party was also a bit different than anything I had ever hosted before. We invited a group of friends over — mostly our age, some family, and some people that we hung out with from work.

I had talked up the party with my work friends the weeks prior and they were all excited. Not only to be getting together but also because I was planning to have some traditional Indian food — samosas and biryani (a rice and meat dish with lots of spices)! Of course, none of my parties are complete without snack trays of cheese, shrimp and barbecue meatballs! Since we were planning on having many "American" friends, we also decided to have some wine and cocktail mixers on hand.

There were two things that surprised me that night at that party, both of which occurred as people entered our home. The first was that a few of the Muslim men would not touch me — no handshake, no hug — just a simple hello. All the Muslim women and our American friends (men and women both) gave me hugs all around!

The second surprising thing was that each of our "American" friends brought over a bottle of wine, while our Muslim friends brought desserts. We laughed later that I had plenty to drink for the whole next year and that we had plenty of dessert for the whole year too! When I think back now, I shouldn't have been so surprised. Muslims do not drink, but no matter what religion or culture you are, it is customary to come to a home bearing a gift.

With those few exceptions, the party was just like any other — people gathered mostly around the food and shared stories of how they knew me versus how they knew Iqbal. Everyone was smiling, laughing and having a good time. It was a great blend of cultures and friends who were all about our age.

A few months later, it was finally time for Iqbal and I to have the whole family — and I mean the *whole* family — over to our house. Since we did not have a big family wedding, I had not had an opportunity to meet many of his family members and certainly had never entertained for them. I was *very* nervous! Our first challenge was picking a date and sending out our invitations. This was easy for the family that was in our generation — we just used Facebook! But to invite the "older" family members, the seemingly simple invitation process meant using Iqbal's mom as an organizer and facilitator. She needed to "grease the wheels" to be sure that we included all the proper aunts, uncles and cousins and that the invitations got out in plenty of time. This was also a special time for me. It was the first Indian party I hosted and with Zulekha helping with the invitations, I wanted to please her and put on a good show as well.

Next came the food. We decided to cater it — I think I'd still be cooking today if I had to make it all on my own! Not only were we trying to determine how much food to get for such a large group (there were going to be 40 people), but where to get it from. We decided to get all (or almost all) Indian food. So began our quest for the best samosas and parathas in town.

We settled on our favorite samosas from Saffron, our biryani from Lazzat Restaurant, our parathas from Pepper and Salt and the rest of the food came from Shahi Nahri. Now while you might think this sounds crazy, Iqbal and I felt we had to make a good impression and wanted to go the extra mile to do it. Not only did we want to get the best food we could find, but due to some of our guest's dietary restrictions, we could only serve Zabiha meats (those that have been Islamically blessed upon their sacrifice). We added some of my favorite party foods to this buffet as well — raw vegetables, cheese and fruit, and a cold shrimp tray. The food was a hit!

Seeing as this was my first real showing for my new family, I needed a new outfit for such a grand affair. American or not, it's a girl thing! Earlier in the year, Iqbal and his mother had taken me to an Indian clothing boutique (Expressions) to get a shalwar kameez for a wedding we were attending. Luckily, at the time, my dear husband insisted on me getting two outfits instead of just one. Well, this worked out perfectly because now I had a second shalwar kameez to wear. Just like American girls, you can't wear the same dress over and over to different parties!

After putting the outfit on, I felt like a princess complete with all the bling — I do like sparkly things, as Iqbal can confirm! I had my hair done for the evening, wore my outfit and had on dangling sparkling diamond earrings (fake ones, darn) and bracelets. Once the other ladies arrived, I fit right in.

As the guests arrived, I was prepared this time for all the hugs from the women and the much more distant hellos from the men. After our last party, I had learned that the men's lack of embrace was not a sign of disrespect to me, but rather a sign of respect for their wives — you don't touch another woman, even if just by handshake. I've learned too that this particular perspective is followed by some (but not all) Muslim men, perhaps depending on their own interpretation and level of faith.

Well, the party went fabulously and I was very delighted as the evening came to a close. As is typical with most family parties, the men had gathered in one part of the house and the women in another. For me, being the outsider (the only white, non-Muslim woman), I was *very* happy to have been accepted and included in all the conversations that evening. As my new found aunts and cousins were leaving, they complimented me again on the delicious food and the wonderful way I looked in my shalwar kameez. Many of them offered to take me shopping to pick out more outfits, which of course I immediately agreed to!

Let's jump back to that Muslim wedding I mentioned a bit ago. On January 1, 2011, I not only attended but participated in a Muslim wedding. It was for Iqbal's cousin, Asra, and her husband, Aamir. Let me tell you, this was an event! The whole affair actually began several days before with the mehndi (kind of like a girl's bachelorette party) at Asra's house. Unfortunately I couldn't go but from my understanding it was a time for the girls to chat, bond and apply henna to their hands and wrists.

Then on Friday, after the regular prayers at the masjid, Asra and Aamir's religious ceremony took place. I took the day off of work and went to witness this special event. I was intrigued as to how exactly the ceremony was going to take place, especially knowing that the women and men sat separately in the prayer hall (more to come in the next chapter).

Well, at the time of the nikah (religious ceremony), the women came downstairs but remained in the back part of the men's prayer hall while the men gathered closer to the front near the Imam. The men did not turn to face or even acknowledge the women and the women sat quietly and solemnly in the back. For the next 30 minutes, the Imam said some prayers, explained the virtues of marriage and asked questions of the groom. Three men then walked over to the bride (who was seated on the floor surrounded by her family and friends) and asked her if she wanted to marry the groom. As I'm told, these men were the witnesses of the marriage. Asra (the bride) did not answer them directly but instead, relayed her agreement through her own witnesses to the men. The three then walked back to Aamir and the Imam and conveyed the message. Thus they were married! There were hugs all around and everyone said, "Mubarak!"

I, of course, was observing all of this with wide wondering eyes. I was so happy to have been invited to witness such an extraordinary event! Although the same happy smiles were on everyone's faces (technically Asra and Aamir were married now), I saw several differences between this wedding and the traditional Christian weddings I had attended in the past. For starters, Asra wore a colorful teal and yellow shalwar kameez as opposed to a long white dress. As the Imam blessed the union between Asra and Aamir, they were sitting several hundred feet apart — practically in separate rooms! For me, this was another learning experience that I was blessed to have been able to share.

The first wedding reception was not until the following day. The Shadi (or bride's reception) was another very unique event in itself. Similar to many other wedding receptions that I had attended, Asra's reception was held in a banquet hall that was decorated with flowing cloths and a stage. On the stage was a gold settee (or love seat) and a side chair. In front of that was a long walk way and to the side of the stage was a podium. The rest of the room was filled with round tables and chairs for all the guests.

For this reception (as opposed to the wedding itself), there were about 18 bridesmaids. I am honored to say that I was one of them. When the festivities began, the girls all lined up and we slowly walked down the center aisle up to the stage, with the last of us being the beautiful bride. Asra had donned a stunning gold and red dress, head covering and lots of bangles. Her makeup and hair were done to perfection. Aamir was in a matching suit also made of gold and red. He had on a traditional Indian turban and even traditional Indian shoes. The two looked as if they had just walked out of a picture book — just amazing! I was in awe!

As with most weddings, there were plenty of pictures of the new bride and groom as they sat side by side on the settee. I couldn't help but just sit back on the side and smile.

This was my first real introduction to the "family." Luckily, my mother-in-law had taken me to the boutique to get the perfect shalwar kameez for the occasion. I had an impression to make! After all, I was not only representing Iqbal as his wife, but I was also the newest member of the Atcha family — Dr. and Mrs. Atcha's new daughter-in-law!

If I wasn't nervous enough at that point, what followed next was a test of my own strength and confidence. I had come to the event with my mother-in-law, who I had assumed would introduce me to all the other members of the family. Well she did, but in doing so, I realized that many of them did not speak English — their native tongue was gujrathi (similar to Urdu and Hindi). Then, just as the introductions were ending, Zulekha found a table with her generation of family members and I was left to find a place to sit by myself. Unfortunately, the few Atcha cousins that I did know had already found seats and their tables were full. Eventually, I found a table that had an empty spot and got to meet some other women.

Now you're probably thinking, "Why didn't you just sit by Iqbal?" Well I would have, but at this particular event, the women did not sit with the men. The aisle that we walked up to the stage with the settee was the dividing line between the men and the women. This was definitely different for me, but then again, it is their culture and their religion and I was the visitor adapting to their ways.

The second wedding reception, called the Valima (or the groom's reception), took place on Sunday. It was held at the same banquet hall and for the most part, the same people attended as the previous night. It's a good thing I had bought that second shalwar kameez because I wore it for this occasion. Unlike the prior evening's Shadi, at this reception the genders could mix, there was music in the background and I was able to sit at a table along with Iqbal and his cousins. Aamir and his family were not quite as strict as his bride had been. I thoroughly enjoyed this whole weekend of festivities and feel truly blessed that I was welcome to share in the events.

As with the wedding and our parties, holidays are full of excitement, family and good food. But unlike the first 40 years of my life, when it comes to holidays I am now asked, "How do you celebrate Christmas? Easter? Thanksgiving?" My answer is simple, "Like I always have!" Being that I am now in an interfaith relationship, that might not necessarily have been the case.

When Iqbal and I were first dating and we came upon our first Christmas, I naturally assumed we would have a traditional holiday season — after all, it was *my* (Christian) holiday. Not thinking anything different than the usual, I envisioned the standard Christmas tree, Christmas stockings, attending Christmas Eve mass and having a special dinner. My thoughts and plans (as they had always been for Christmas) were that we would wake up on Christmas morning and open gifts. Of course, there would be plenty of them to go around! So for our first year together, that is exactly what I had planned to do.

Little did I know that Iqbal had never really celebrated Christmas this way. I knew he had celebrated Christmas before with his other in-laws, but it never occurred to me that he had never actually had a Christmas tree in his own house!

Well, it was time for a change … for him! We had agreed early on in our marriage that we were not going to "convert" each other to our respective faiths, nor were we going to require that each other forgo their own. I took that to mean the traditions and habits connected therewith, such as Christmas and Easter. Unfortunately, due to the proverbial "lack of communication," this also lead to one of our first arguments — now playfully referred to as "Trees, Beer and Marriage."

In an e-mail (appropriately titled), I wrote the following:

Okay — so perhaps it didn't hit me last night while we were first talking. But this morning, after some thought, I am left very confused and conflicted. It is as much the specific issues, as the concepts and perhaps even the way they were discussed.

As for the specifics, it is not a tree … that is the issue, but what they represent. The tree is a part of Christmas, Christmas is a part of celebrating Jesus's birth, Jesus is a part of what I (and Kimmy) believe and celebrate.… Giving up that tree, and the celebration of Christmas, would be to me like denouncing my faith. I cannot do that.

I would like you to share in the Christmas celebration to the extent that you wish, just as you did Easter. However, I am not willing to "give it up" as a condition/consolation of marriage to you or anyone. I am not asking you to believe what I believe, and I am not asking you to change your beliefs. I am asking, or rather expecting, that you will respect my faith and its customs, as I will respect yours.

You see, when we first discussed Christmas, I naturally assumed we would have a tree. It was only a matter of where we would put it in the living room. However, his exact response was, "I'm not sure about having a tree." Of course, I took this to mean there was a possibility that we wouldn't have one!

In my highly emotional state of feeling like I was being told, "No," and also feeling like he was discounting my faith, I naturally saw this simple statement as a huge obstacle. That crushing feeling led me to write that e-mail (and much more anxiety than I cared for). I loved Iqbal and I loved what we were building together in terms of a family and a life — but this! This was a total shock! It had never occurred to me that we would not have a Christmas tree. Even more so, it never occurred to me that we would even be discussing the *possibility* of not having a Christmas tree. Rightly so, I was very, very upset. Would it have been a "deal breaker" to our relationship? I think so. No, let me re-phrase that … *I know so!*

As is evident by the fact that we are still together and writing this book, I eventually calmed down. Over the next several days, we talked things out and we both realized how essential communication is and that words alone can join (or tear apart) two worlds.

As you can imagine, the kids had no problems at all celebrating Christmas — it was great to receive "extra" gifts. Since Haroon and Hassanah had never put up a Christmas tree, they were excited with the decorations, the music, the hot chocolate and all the laughs. We made it into a true family affair. Since Christmas is not just a "Hallmark holiday," both Kim and I tried to teach Iqbal and his kids the real story behind Christmas — that of the birth of Jesus.

Easter and Eid were next on the list, and each of these days was accompanied by the joys of giving (and receiving) gifts as well as the lessons and history behind each holiday. I have always loved holidays and celebrations. To me, giving gifts — big or small — and sharing love with family and friends is what life is all about.

Lessons Learned

Be confident in yourself as you
participate in new experiences.

Be humble and respectful of other people's customs.

No matter what culture you are from, all men talk
politics and all women talk clothes and jewelry.

CHAPTER 8

Prayer and Worship

Before we started dating, Amy and I never really talked about religion. I knew she was Christian because of the gold cross pendant she wore to Tae Kwon Do. My guess was that she knew that I was Muslim because I didn't go to class during Ramadan and because I didn't drink alcohol at any of our friends' parties.

Neither of us saw religion or race as a condition of friendship but as we grew closer, we started asking more and more questions about each other's faith. We weren't looking to convert or to be converted, but we wanted to understand each other's beliefs and find the similarities between them. There was a lot to share and we were eager to learn as well.

It wasn't long before we got our first opportunity. It came soon after I had bought the house. Whenever Amy came over for dinner, I'd always ask her to take off her shoes in the doorway before coming in. I don't think she understood why at first, but she was polite and always did. It was ok to wear shoes inside her house, which felt very weird to me, but I was insistent we would take them off in mine ... uh, ours.

In most Indian, Arab and Eastern cultures, people remove their shoes before walking into a house as a sign of respect and good hygiene.

If you think about it, your shoes come in contact with a lot of nasty things: mud, leaves, gum, and poop to name a few. It's a pretty gross world we walk in and to track all that garbage inside the house would make it equally as dirty.

Keeping my house clean and neat is a priority for me (and not just because I have undiagnosed OCD). If you've ever heard the phrase "cleanliness is next to Godliness," you'll understand that it goes hand in hand with being a Muslim. Having a clean house to pray in is a must and I wanted to be sure that I had that. It was new to Amy at first and she forgot a couple of times, but we kept at it. Within a few months, she knew the drill and soon enough, she was reminding guests to leave their shoes at the door too!

Purity and cleanliness are a big part of faith. Having a nice, clean home is one thing, but being nice and clean yourself is just as important. It goes without saying that Amy and I shower regularly, but a Muslim does more than that before saying his five daily prayers. One afternoon, Amy walked into the bathroom to find my foot in the sink! There I was in a polo shirt and rolled up jeans with my head, hands and arms dripping wet. She just stood there for a second, smiled and waited.

I explained that I was doing wudhu (Arabic for ablution) and that it was a ritual I had to do before I could pray or touch the Quran. Wudhu is pretty much like a baptism except that we do it on a regular basis and it doesn't involve full body immersion. Amy could relate because whenever she entered her church, she would dip her fingers in holy water and touch her forehead, heart and both shoulders. The concept was the same, but the practice was different. That wasn't always the case.

When Amy and I visited Italy, we visited the Piazza del Duomo (also known as Cathedral Square) in Pisa. Our tour guide explained to us in great detail that the three main structures of the Piazza (the Baptistery, the Cathedral and the Cemetery) symbolized the three stages of a Christian's life. Before parishioners could offer their prayers in the Cathedral, they had to enter the Baptistery first and wash themselves in order to be pure.

Back in the days of Galileo, you couldn't enter the house of God impure and unclean. It was a violation of the church and you would be looked upon as insolent and disrespectful. The church has changed quite a bit since then and the way followers of both faiths perform ablution or wudhu isn't the same. Regardless, it's plain to see the value water has for both Muslims and Christians in purifying the body and soul overall.

The more we talked, the more things we learned we had in common between our faiths and our cultures. Both our parents raised us to believe that attending service was very special ... and very mandatory! When we were kids, they stressed to us that it wasn't just an opportunity to get closer to God, but to make friends and build relationships with other kids like us. Of course, when we were kids, none of that mattered. All Amy and I remembered was that our moms and dads made us get up earlier than we wanted to, take a shower, scrub behind our ears, put on some very spiffy but itchy clothes, sit in church or masjid and that they'd get mad at us every time we talked during the priest or imam's speech!

Needless to say, we owe our parents a lot because we still wake up early, shower, put on our best clothes and drive to church or masjid. We've gotten good at washing behind the ears but our nice clothing is more comfortable to wear.

I had been to a church many times before I met Amy but it was always for a funeral, a wedding, or a baptism. I had even been asked to be a godfather for two Catholic friends many years ago and had graciously accepted the honor. Still, I had never sat through an entire Sunday Mass and I had a lot of questions about why Catholics did what they did. My professors at Loyola had shared with me the life and teachings of Christ, but very little about the Church.

I had no idea what rituals they followed or what the reasons were behind them. On the flipside, the only masjid Amy had ever been to was a mosque in Tunisia as part of a sight-seeing tour. She knew we both worshipped one God but she had never been to a Friday mass (called Jumma Salaat) and she had no idea about anything else. So we decided the best way to learn was to attend Sunday Mass and Jumma Salaat together.

On a bright and crisp September morning, Amy and I drove to St. Luke's parish in Carol Stream, Illinois. She had been talking up Father Schutter's homilies (what I call sermons) for the past two months and I was excited about my first Sunday experience. As we entered, Amy knelt and made "the sign of the cross" using holy water. She led me to the pew she had sat in for the past 20 years and I flipped through the book of hymns and readings while waiting for mass to begin.

The church was definitely smaller and less "glitzy" than the cathedrals I had visited before, but the organ music and gigantic cross were exactly the same. When a parishioner stood and rang a bell three times to signal the start of mass, I couldn't help but crack up watching all the parents gather their nicely dressed children and telling them to be quiet. Ah, memories!

The differences between Sunday mass and Jumma Salaat were easy to pick out. Music played throughout mass, men and women sat and sang together, people took communion and then there was the hand holding. Apparently, Catholics hold hands during the "Our Father" prayer and while I've held hands with Amy a million times before, holding a total stranger's hand for a few minutes was … let's just say new. It was interesting to experience the differences but I couldn't help noticing the similarities as well.

The priest recited scripture for at least ten minutes before starting his sermon and the congregation did a lot of sitting, standing and kneeling (which one parishioner sweetly referred to as "popcorn"). After the sermon, prayers were made for specific parishioners, the sick and the oppressed and members of the congregation greeted each other with the phrase "peace be with you." It was heart-warming to say the least and the familiar vibe of brotherly love was in the air. As I watched parents give their children money and then instruct them to put it in the offering plate, I couldn't help but remember how my father had done the same to me and I had done the same for my kids. Small world indeed!

So when Amy decided to take the plunge and visit a masjid with me, I sat down to prepare her a little. The rules of visiting a masjid were a bit more defined than going to church. I bought Amy a hijab (head scarf) and helped her practice putting it on. I explained to her that Christianity, Judaism and Islam all required women to cover their hair before entering a house of worship and she was fine with it. It was when I started to give her directions on how to get to the women's area that made her raise her eyebrows.

Amy had just assumed I would be sitting with her the whole time, giving play by play details about the khutbah (Islamic sermon). In the masjid, men and women sit separately to avoid (what I call) the "distraction of attraction" phenomena. I promised her she'd be OK and the very next Friday, off we went to Jumma Salaat. There are three masjids near our house, but I took her to the one where my kids went to school: Islamic Foundation. It was the biggest, most beautiful and diverse masjid in our area! We walked in and after reminding her to take off her shoes, I told her I'd meet her after salaat by the car. She was excited to share with me what she saw and I won't spoil her surprise. You can read all about it in her part of the chapter.

There were a lot of little things that made us stop and take notice as well. For example, Amy pointed out that some Muslims use a rosary after every prayer. It's something I used to do when I was little but I wasn't aware that Catholics use one too! Even though ours has 100 beads and a Catholic rosary has 59, we both use it to praise God and recite specific prayers in each section.

Another common practice in both religions is tithing or Zakat. Every year at the beginning of Ramadan, I'll sit down and calculate our savings from last Ramadan and divide it by half (since Amy and I make about the same). I then donate 2.5 percent to a charitable organization dedicated to feeding orphans, the poor or some other needy souls. Christians of all denominations are asked to give (up to) 10 percent of their gross income directly to the Church. Amy isn't as particular to the percentage as I am, but donating on a regular basis to the masjid, the church and charitable organizations continues to purify our wealth and help those who suffer.

Finding similarities in our faith didn't always have us high-fiving each other. One of the more challenging requirements in both our faiths was Ramadan and Lent. Amy hadn't seen me fast before and she got her first dose of it after we were married. Let me just say, it's taken her a few years to adjust. Since I turned eight, I've observed Ramadan every year, and am used to not eating or drinking anything (even water) during the day. In my twenties, I learned to avoid smoking and marital relations as well.

It's not easy to get through the day without those things but you learn to make do. After a few days, your body gets tired and you start to talk less in order to reserve your strength. This didn't settle well with Amy. She was used to my fun-loving and outgoing personality and was quick to point out that I was "crabby and short-tempered," which only added to my crabbiness and short-temperedness. It happens year after year and I'll remind her that my energy level is low, so the best thing for me to do is to keep silent. Sometimes it works and she'll leave me alone but sometimes, she'll keep pointing it out.

The other "major" impact Ramadan has had on Amy is my sleep cycle. For the past few years, Ramadan has been starting earlier in the year, moving from fall into summer. That's because it's based on the lunar calendar and it's 11 days shorter than the Gregorian calendar. As a result, fasting begins earlier in the morning and ends later at night. The extra nightly prayers I read as well guarantee that my head doesn't hit the pillow till well past 11:00 PM. Amy and I used to fall asleep at 9:00 PM, but during Ramadan there's no hope of any snuggling or "husband-wife" activities.

It's an annual challenge we face and we've learned to schedule some nights where I don't eat a full dinner in order to spend time with each other in bed. Still, it isn't enough for either of us. I'm sure it will be much easier in 20 years when Ramadan starts in December. I just hope my drive will be as strong when I'm 60 as it is today!

On the flipside, Lent at our house isn't nearly as taxing. Every year, Amy announces that she's either going to give up desserts or she's going to start working out ... again. It's very different from what I do in Ramadan and it's also a lot less strict than what my Jesuit friends at Loyola had taught me. It used to get under my skin because (as Amy's husband), I wanted her to practice her faith as best as she could.

Call it a case of "religious jealousy" but with what Ramadan requires, I believe that God requires a greater sacrifice. The more powerful the struggle, the greater appreciation God has for it. But as I witness this year after year, I am reminded that my viewpoints about her religious observance are things I can't change. It's Amy's choice to observe Lent the way she finds it most comfortable.

Prayer and Worship

Personal, intimate, peaceful — that's what comes to mind when I think of Jesus and God. Every day I pray, I learn more about myself, my existence in this world and my relationship with my fellow man. When I watch Iqbal pray, whether it is together at the table before a meal or by himself while on his "janamaz" (prayer rug) facing Mecca, I see the similarities in our basic beliefs about God.

Our faith is one of the most fascinating things for me to reflect on when I think about my relationship with Iqbal. We are definitely different — he is Muslim and I am Catholic. But the more I get to know him and learn about Islam, the more I see the similarities in the traditions and practices of our two religions.

The first time I went to masjid (the prayer hall) with Iqbal, I was curious and quite nervous. I wasn't frightened from the concern that "these Muslim people" would immediately "hate" me for being a Christian, but rather that I would do something that was offensive to them due to my own ignorance. I would gladly have just "shadowed" Iqbal in the prayer hall and sat patiently next to him listening, watching and absorbing. Unfortunately, that wasn't the case.

In the Muslim world, women pray separately from the men. This is done so that both groups can be more focused in their faith and respect than if they were mixed with the opposite sex, which might distract them. In the few mosques that I have been to, the women sat on a different floor — either upstairs in a balcony or on the lower level or basement, while the men sat on the main floor. In one small mosque that I attended in Austin, Texas, the women prayed at the back of the room separated only by drapery from ceiling to floor. Women typically cannot see the Imam directly, but may have a view by way of a TV monitor or may simply be able to listen to the sermon.

Upon entering the mosque, everyone — men, women and children — is required to take off their shoes. At first, I didn't know the reason for this other than to not track dirt. Now, however, I have come to understand that worshippers perform a "cleansing" of their body (referred to as "wudhu") prior to prayer. This cleansing of the hands, feet and face is a sign of respect that the person is "clean" and "pure" enough to pray to God. In some mosques that I have been in, their bathrooms had an extra area for this cleansing process. While watching the other women one Friday afternoon, I thought to myself that this time spent washing and cleansing makes sense as a way of peacefully centering your mind for prayer. I wondered if this was anything like crossing myself with the holy water?

Salaat (the Islamic term for the formal prayers) starts with the "call to prayer" that is the most well-known practice in the Muslim faith. When I walked into the prayer hall as the call was ending, both men and women scrambled through the doors, quickly taking their places in the large room. At this same time, I noticed that the women who are already there and "settled in" were doing their own silent prayers, following the same ritualistic movements that I had seen Iqbal do when he was at home praying.

From the back row where I sat, I looked out at the group of women before me. Each sat closely to the next in lines that were literally made as part of the carpet facing towards Mecca. There were no pews or benches. All the women and most of the girls (some as young as seven or eight years) had on a "hijab" or head scarf. I looked and saw that the scarves ranged from plain white to brilliant colors and while some matched their outfits, others did not. The women's hair was tucked into their scarves, with some tightly wound around their faces. Many of the women also left their coats on or wore long robes to cover their clothes. I had my head scarf on too, although I seemed to keep re-wrapping it several times to prevent it from slipping down my head.

A few minutes later, the women all sat down on the carpet and an Imam began the sermon. Most of the time when I had gone to masjid, the sermon had been said in English, as it was on my first visit. Other times (depending on who the Imam was), it was given in Urdu (which I do not speak) and left me feeling more than a little lost.

Since this sermon was in English, I listened closely to the message and noticed something very intriguing. For this (and almost every visit I've made since), the general message that was being shared was one of loving thy neighbor, respecting others and God and generally behaving as a good person should in order to go to heaven. With the exception that they used the words Allah and Muhammad, the message could almost have been the same as in any Christian church I have attended!

After the lesson was told, the women lined up shoulder to shoulder across the lines on the carpet and prayed in unison. Although I couldn't see it, I believed the same was happening on the floor with the men. Their prayers were still basically silent, being led only by the Imam. However, they were now all unified through their actions. The children were encouraged to pray right next to their moms too, standing tall in their own spot, shoulder to shoulder with the next.

Now that the newness of this experience (and my accompanying nervousness) have lessened, I am able to sit peacefully during the sermon with my eyes closed and concentrate on what is being said rather than where I am at. I'll admit though, that sometimes the accent of the Imam can make it difficult for me to understand. After visiting the masjid and especially comparing it to my own church, I have gained an ever-increasing sense of respect and appreciation that we are all here on this earth spreading the same word of God — even though it is in our own different ways.

Although I have watched Iqbal pray on several occasions at home and have been invited to pray with the women at the masjid, I have always been reluctant to do so. "Why?" you might ask — especially since I just told you that the sermon is really not so different than at my Catholic mass. For whatever reason, I just don't feel comfortable doing so because it is not my faith. I am a guest in their "house" and would prefer to respectfully just sit and listen.

When I go for prayers, I always sit at the back of the room on the chairs that line the wall or on the carpet itself. Iqbal had told me during one of our first discussions about Islam that women who were having their menstrual cycle are not required to pray but may go to the masjid anyway — thus the chairs at the back of the room.

At the time of that discussion, this concept in itself was new and very confusing to me. My initial reaction was not very positive. I did not understand the nuances of "not required to pray" versus "not allowed to pray," which is what I had thought Iqbal had meant. This misunder-standing, again based on simple miscommunication, lead to another one of our more notable arguments.

From Iqbal's comment, I believed that Muslim women who were menstruating were not "clean enough" to pray before God. I was furious! How could that be? After all, God had created women to have a men-strual cycle. Why then would He not want them to pray no matter what time of the month it was?! Now, I felt that I *really* did not understand his faith! I thought for a few brief moments, "Aha! This is exactly what I've always heard — Muslims treat women as secondary ... not allowing them to pray! Hrmph!"

Lucky for me, Iqbal is a very patient man. When I had calmed down, he explained to me that yes, it is a matter of "not being clean." But more importantly, it should be viewed from the point that women are "excused from the requirement" to pray during this time. It took me a while to grasp this concept, especially because I don't believe that prayer is or should be a "requirement" but rather a desire — thus my confusion. It's all in the matter of understanding from two different perspectives.

One other day when I attended the masjid with Iqbal, I noticed a woman praying with some beads. At first, I was confused — I thought she had a rosary! After watching her a while longer, I realized that this small colorful bracelet was in fact a set of prayer beads. However, it was slightly different from my traditional rosary. Her Muslim prayer beads were similar in size and shape, but did not have the cross on the end (obviously). Like my Catholic rosaries, Muslim prayer beads can be found in many colors and styles. It's interesting that I happened to notice this woman's because as of late, I have found myself collecting rosaries from various places I've visited — Vatican City, Warsaw, Poland and Assisi, Italy. Whether I say the prayers or not, the rosary brings me a sense of peace and calmness whenever I hold it. It seemed to do that for the woman too.

I enjoy going to masjid with Iqbal, although I don't often get the opportunity to go. The holy day for Muslims is Friday and the main prayer is around noon (although the time fluctuates here in the U. S. due to daylight saving time). It's my understanding that the masjid is open seven days a week for all five prayers each day. Since I typically work Monday through Friday, I am not able to go unless I happen to take the day off.

Prayer at home for Iqbal is about the same as it is in the masjid, at least from what I can tell. Iqbal will wait until the "call to prayer" is complete, do his "wudhu," then lay out a janamaz on the ground in the living room or some other quiet place in the house, making sure it always faces Mecca. A few years ago, I bought Iqbal an Azan clock — it tells the time of the five prescribed prayers and announces or sounds the call to prayer at the beginning of each.

Over the years, the kids, myself, and yes, even the cat, have become accustomed to the Azan and to Iqbal doing his prayers in the living room. During this time, we try to be quiet out of respect for him and for God. However, if I am busy and being a bit noisy, Iqbal will go to a bedroom or downstairs. At first, I used to feel bad about this as if I was bothering him. But now, I believe that our worlds need to blend and sometimes that means him finding a quiet place as opposed to the rest of the house having to be silent to accommodate him (even if it is only for five to ten minutes). Most times when Iqbal is done with his prayers, he will kiss me on the head and then continue with whatever he was doing before. Admittedly, I have also found that the Azan works as an excellent "extra alarm clock" since it coincides with my usual wake-up time on many weekday mornings — sigh!

As for church, I go rather regularly and Iqbal has joined me on a few occasions. Unlike masjid, however, he gets to sit next to me! On the days that he goes, he seems to listen intently to the speakers and the priest and observes all that is going on around him. Understandably (although not necessarily appropriately), he consistently leans over to ask me questions about what is going on and the significance of certain events. I have tried to be patient with his learning, but sometimes I think I have a small child with me that I have to constantly remind that talking during mass is a "no-no"!

As you might expect, clothing at my church is conservative. Ever since I was a child, I was taught that a person should "wear their Sunday best" for church. But my mother also taught me that God does not care so much about what you are wearing as He does the fact that you attend mass. With this being said, you must always remember to show respect for yourself, others and the church. Thus no shorts or tank tops are allowed and your knees and shoulders should be covered. In today's age, no hats or veils are required, but this wasn't always the case. Perhaps this rule was not so different than a hijab.

What I really love about going to prayers or mass together with Iqbal is the philosophical and intellectual conversations that stem from the sermon. If we have time, we go to lunch afterwards and continue our discussions about life, the sermon, and the practical ways we can apply what we have just learned to our everyday world. It truly is amazing to me how much we can talk about our own faith (both as discussion and teaching) as well as about religion and life in general after we have listened.

In talking about masjid and prayers with Iqbal, I learned a few of the more basic differences in practice between our faiths. For example, there is not necessarily one assigned Imam at a masjid, nor is there any particular set of prescribed readings or sermon for a particular week. This is very different from the Catholic Church. At every church I have ever attended (from childhood until today), the priest at the parish had been assigned there by the Diocese and served as the primary (and sometimes only) priest in that church for as long as the Diocese dictated. Thus the priest turned into "my priest" and was similar to a father figure or elder relative for many of us growing up and throughout the years.

At a Catholic mass (no matter what time of day or even location), every mass has the same elements with three designated readings for that particular day — one from the Old Testament, one from the New Testament and one from the Gospel. So, just as it was when I went to Poland, the readings, songs and cadence are so familiar that I can tell exactly where we are in the service (even if I don't speak the language).

What about the seating arrangements? If you are Muslim you might ask, "How is it that you pray all mixed together — men and women?" In my church, families sit all together, sometimes taking up an entire pew. We believe that a family that prays together stays together, so to speak. So Mom, Dad and all the kids will sit in the same pew. In some churches, there is a "crying room" for the babies. However at St. Luke Parish, where I have been going for the past 20 years, children and adults alike sit side by side. In many churches (including mine) we hold hands while saying the "Our Father" prayer and offer each other the sign of peace — usually a handshake or perhaps a hug and kiss between parent and child. We pray as one large community with Christ.

The only other outward and everyday difference I could tell between Islam and Catholicism is that our dedicated holy day is Sunday. But like the masjid, my Catholic church is open for prayer almost every day of the week.

In addition to the more routine weeks of prayer, there are special celebrations such as Lent and Easter, Ramadan and Eid. While the underlying premise of each of these events is different, the worship and its culmination in a joyous celebration cannot be overlooked.

Each year as the season approaches, I can't help but notice the rituals and customs of my Lenten time (which end on Easter Sunday) and compare that with Iqbal's observance of Ramadan and its ending on Eid. Sure, the more materialistic Easter Bunny with its scattering of eggs and big basket of candies is part of the more Americanized tradition, but look at it instead from the religious view. On both occasions, it's a time for reflection, a time for thought and penance and a time for gratitude. In observing either Lent or Ramadan, the followers of the faith are required to fast, abstain from exuberance and try to be more connected with God. This time of concentrated faith (40 days for Lent; 30 days of Ramadan) is then rewarded with a glorious celebration — Easter or Eid! It's another occasion to celebrate with family and friends over the joys in life that God shares with us.

Even with the fundamental differences in beliefs, our faiths, just like us humans, are really not so very far apart.

Lessons Learned

☪ ✝

Respect each other's beliefs, especially
when you don't agree with them.

It's okay to share in another's practice of
worship. You're not denouncing your own.

There are plenty of similarities between Islam
and Catholicism, if you look for them.

CHAPTER 9

Our Life Continues ...

The more places we go, the more we hear people ask us, "What's it like being an interfaith/interracial couple?" After five years, my answer is still the same: it's normal! I don't see our marriage being anything different than any other couple. We both have our issues with each other that make us mad or upset. She thinks I'm a neat freak and I think she goes shopping too much. But then we talk it over, we kiss and then we make up.

We've come to understand that certain things make us happy and because we love each other, we just let the other person do it. That took us a few years to learn but we got that down pretty good. Raising our kids together wasn't as hard as you'd think either.

When Amy and I got married, Haroon was 15, Kim was 13 and Hassanah was 12. They were all practically teenagers and while they still had a lot to learn about life, they were old enough to know the basics. I'm talking about all the things we had taught them growing up like being polite and respectful, speaking clearly, picking up after yourself, taking a shower, cleaning your room, etc. If you've ever dealt with teenagers, I'm sure you know where I'm coming from. For the most part, it was your everyday parent/teenager battles that took place at the Atcha house, but religion and race were never an issue.

We had been pretty clear from the get-go that I was still going to raise Haroon and Hassanah as Muslim and Amy would still raise Kim as Catholic. The kids knew their own religion well enough to practice it but weren't shy about learning something new about another faith. From time to time, Amy and I would find ourselves to be too busy to oversee something and we'd ask each other for help.

When I was at work, Amy would remind Haroon and Hassanah to pray and when Amy was busy, I would take Kim to church for catechism. Other than that, there was little crossover in raising our children Muslim or Catholic the way they had been brought up. Haroon's in college now and both Kim and Hassanah are graduating from high school this year. Time flies very quickly and with the ups and downs of teenagers, I'm sure we have a few more years of stress ahead of us as they enter their twenties.

We've been asked a couple of times how we'd raise a baby if we had one of our own. I am blessed to say that we will never have to worry about that unless God decides to perform a miracle. I can guarantee that neither of us would have given up our right to raise a baby in our own faith or tradition, but helping to raise someone else's baby in their respective faith isn't an issue.

Not everyone we knew had questions about our marriage. We've had a few people in our lives who decided to walk away entirely. Some had been friends for decades and others were close-knit family members. I had expected it from some in the older generation but I was pretty surprised that there were a few from my generation. I don't take it personally though.

People have a different tolerance level for strangers, acquaintances, friends and spouses. You're OK if you stay in the circle but if you cross the line and try to move up, that's not OK. Some had a difficult time accepting us because of our different faiths and others because of our heritage. We even had one priest ask us how we could Biblically justify being married. He couldn't wrap his mind around how two people could live in the same house if they didn't believe the same thing. I've tried not to laugh out loud when I hear things like that, but I know plenty of families that are both liberals and conservatives, Democrats and Republicans, gay and straight, black, white, mixed and other. We live in a very diverse world and the only way to get along is to show tolerance and respect to everyone.

That's where one of the biggest changes came in our lives. After my father and I buried the hatchet, Amy and I started spending more time with my parents. We have breakfast with them twice a month now and if I'm not traveling, I try to spend an hour every day with them.

They're getting older and I realize how valuable having your parents' love and support really is. We've added a couple of new traditions besides spending Christmas and Eid together. For the past few years, Amy and I have been celebrating Mother's Day and Father's Day together with our moms and dads. It's cute to see my mom and Amy's mom together because they both love to talk, both like to travel and they're both "vertically challenged." But when you see these two ladies walking side by side like friends, it's an amazing feeling to know that friendship doesn't see color or race either.

So what's life like for me and Amy today? Well, Amy still works 14 hours a day and I still travel around the country for my job. We're actively involved in several organizations and we still attend church and masjid regularly. Life keeps moving forward and as our parents have gotten older, we've come to accept that we will be taking care of them when they no longer can.

That doesn't stop us from having our date nights and from spreading our message of love, tolerance and respect. We have a lot of plans and dreams for making the world a better place and I really believe that over the next few years, we'll be successful in doing just that.

Being an interracial and interfaith couple wasn't something Amy and I set out to do. We were just two people who became friends and fell in love. Amy and I talk to each other and exercise a lot of patience when we don't understand why the other does (or won't do) something. It's helped us deal with our own limitations and it's helped us create a safe and loving environment for both of us to live our own lives while still respecting each other's beliefs.

That's the thing about love and friendship. It doesn't see color, race, or religion and it can be created and nurtured by anyone in the world. Our desire to learn from each other and accept one another for who we are has helped make us stronger, both individually and as a couple.

Our Life Continues ...

✝

It still surprises me how often I am asked, "How do things work in a Muslim/Catholic marriage?" When posed with the question, I'm still taken aback at first, but I am reluctant to be so flippant as to say, "The same way every marriage works!" But, it's true! Being a part of an interfaith/interracial marriage really is no different than any other relationship between two people — each person is in fact his/her own person and there must always be a level of respect, even in disagreements.

You may have noticed that there is one section in this book that we did not directly address — children. To give you the long and short of it, for Iqbal and myself, our decision regarding this subject was easier than for most. Since ours was a second marriage for both of us and we each had at least one child from our first marriage, we opted not to have any more kids. In hindsight, this was probably a good thing and certainly the "easy" way out of dealing with this issue.

From the very beginning of our relationship, Iqbal and I had the understanding that we are both very strong in our faith and that we were not going to try to convert each other. The same held true for our children. Thus, Kim is still being raised Catholic and Haroon and Hassanah are still being raised Muslim. Kim still attends mass with me when she can. We celebrate Easter and Christmas and try to act in a "Christian" way. I have raised her to believe in God and Jesus, to trust God when she is conflicted, give thanks often, and to ask for His help when in need. She has a Bible (like I do) near her bed, although neither of us read from it regularly. I have raised her to abstain from sex until she is married and (luckily) have never had to remind her to dress modestly.

Our children will always be an important part of our lives. But now that they are in their late teens and ready to go out into the world, Iqbal and I can focus more on "our" life together.

One comment that Hassanah made several years ago stuck with me though. On an evening when we just happened to be discussing intercultural relationships, Hassanah rather profoundly blurted out, "Eventually the whole world will be taupe." This phrase was brilliant, seeing how insightful it was *and* how this younger generation is not so caught up in all the racial and cultural differences that existed in our past. All three of the kids have gone to school with so many other kids of different faiths and cultures that it just seems natural for them to have friends of all kinds.

I'm not sure what we would have done had Iqbal and I had a child together. We are both very strong in our respective faiths and it would have been a challenge as to how to raise our child. Perhaps this is an example of how "God works in mysterious ways" and why I believe that "all things happen the way they do for a reason."

As for our home life, Iqbal and I continue to acknowledge and respect each other's beliefs and preferences. This applies both in terms of faith and culture but more importantly, just as different people. We continue to learn and share every day with some new piece of news or insight.

Over our short five years of marriage, we have definitely had our ups and downs. So much is new when two people get together but added to the twists and turns that life brings, even a single day can turn into a drama! Compromise and communication are key. We've learned that most of our disagreements come from one of us not truly or not completely expressing our thoughts and actions.

While we are still learning about each other, we continue to teach and remind our parents that their child still holds fast to the religious beliefs and cultural traditions in which they were raised since birth. It's funny (to me at least) that even in my mid-forties, I need to remind my mom that just because I wear a shalwar kameez to a party or attend masjid with Iqbal for Eid, it does not mean that I have abandoned my own faith or that I have adopted his. Similarly, I've had to remind Iqbal's parents (in my own subtle way), that I am quite happy with my own religion and have no intention or desire to convert to Islam.

I learn about life by participating as much as by reading and watching. As Iqbal will attest, everything is an adventure and an experience for me. We have been fortunate to travel and see the world — the vast and unending miles of nature — on both land and water; the wondrous man-made treasures on earth and the ones hand-chosen by God Himself. We've sampled the "good life," the tastes, the smells and the touch of other cultures — different from either of our own — and yet, we still crave more. I hope I always remain the "sponge" that I am, absorbing every last bit of knowledge for which I am forever grateful to have been given.

From an outsider's point of view, you may not ever guess that we are an interfaith couple. We just continue on with life the way we always have, loving, learning and respecting each other.

Lessons Learned

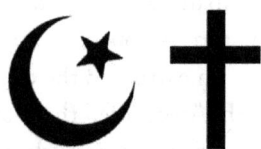

☾ ✚

Never stop living.

Never stop loving.

Never stop respecting.

Afterword

According to a 2008 Pew Research Center Report and the Pew Forum on Religion and Public Life, 15 percent of all new U. S. marriages are interracial and 37 percent of all U. S. marriages are interfaith. That's a huge jump from the civil rights era of the 1960s. It is our belief that with advancing technology and increasing global migration, people will begin to see more similarities between themselves and others and these numbers will rise around the world.

This book was not meant to be a source of information regarding Catholicism or Islam. There are plenty of resources available for you to learn the details of either faith. However, we hope that this story shed some light on how two people of different religions and cultures can work with their differences rather than against them.

While we've presented it in the form of our marriage, Amy and I firmly believe that bridging differences between people can extend beyond a household. It can (and should) work for relationships on the job and at school, with friends, your neighbors and even with people you simply meet on the street.

So where can you start? The best place to begin is with the people closest to you — your family. While most of them practice the same religious and cultural traditions that you do, they may know someone who is different. It may be someone of a different faith or someone of a different culture — or both! Ask to learn more about who that person is and then contact them. Meet them for coffee or lunch to learn more about them.

When you do, listen to that person. Be sure to clear your mind and take the time to truly hear them. Always remember to respect their journey and their beliefs, even if you don't agree. Listen, don't judge. Remember, this is a learning process — the more you listen, the more they will be willing to share.

If you happen to find someone that converted to a new faith or moved to a new country, ask that person why. Find out what made them want to change — what they like about their new faith or way of life and what differences they have found. At the same time, find out what didn't work for them in their old way. Ask them questions and listen to their stories. Be sincere. Don't stop them short or be defensive — especially if their thinking is not the same as yours.

Then there are your friends. Your paths have crossed for a reason. If they are different then you — this is a golden opportunity to learn something completely new. Having already established a sense of trust with a friend, they're more likely to share their beliefs and traditions openly and willingly — but only if you ask! Show a genuine interest. Again, remember to listen with respect and humility — you are here to learn, not judge.

Spend time with your friend at his or her house and observe what they do and how they do it. Many times, family members from an older generation who live in the house do not speak the same language and they will communicate in their native tongue. Even though you may not understand, watch how they interact. See the traditional elements in their home and ask about their meanings. The more interest you show, the more they will invite you to become a part of their traditions. Families of all walks of life are happy, even proud, to share their heritage and will be more apt to do so in their own home with a guest.

Visiting a religious or cultural community center is another great way to explore unfamiliar worlds. The priest, imam, rabbi or religious leader may not be your first point of contact, but there are plenty of people who volunteer at the center and would be willing to speak with you firsthand and explain their practices. Exploring and observing the rituals at a religious or cultural center is a sign of respect and people of all walks of life understand that.

Finally, the best way to learn is to be fully immersed in an environment where that particular culture or religion is the predominant way of life. When Amy and I visited Italy, we were shocked to witness how diverse different regions and cities were. In our "American" way of thinking, we just assumed that every city and its citizens were the same. What remained constant was the church's role in the community and in the lives of its people.

Watching movies like *Under the Tuscan Sun* gives you a small glimpse of what life could be like. But to get a guided tour of an olive farmer's ranch, to taste her food and celebrate with Italians the way they do ... there is no comparison! Guided tour companies (e.g., Globus) offer many packages that fit a variety of budgets and restrictions. To live, breathe, and experience life the way others do builds that connection with other people. When you are the stranger in a strange land, it makes you want to fit in. For a few days or a few weeks, your mindset changes, and slowly but surely, you begin to see what life is like through their eyes. You meet people who eat, pray and love differently than you do.

Getting to know someone doesn't take a lot of preparation or know how. Simply smile and say hello to everyone you meet. A genuine smile is neither small nor insignificant. Amy has a wonderful saying, "If you see a friend without a smile, give them one of yours!"

People will always open their hearts and take a chance when they feel safe, loved and welcomed. We all live on one planet and the more we get to know people from around the world, the more likely we will help our worlds converge. Bridging differences is all about learning, sharing and respecting others.

To have peace, we must believe we already have it and act accordingly. Christians, Muslims and people of all faiths just want the same things: love, peace and security. If we all acted in a gentle and loving manner, it would automatically invite others to act in the same way. Everyone can live in peace with each other — we just have to be willing to converge our worlds.

Footprints in the Sand
Mary Stevenson

One night a man had a dream. He dreamed
he was walking along the beach with the LORD.

Across the sky flashed scenes from his life.
For each scene he noticed two sets of
footprints in the sand: one belonging
to him, and the other to the LORD.

When the last scene of his life flashed before him,
he looked back at the footprints in the sand.

He noticed that many times along the path of
his life there was only *one* set of footprints.

He also noticed that it happened at the very
lowest and saddest times in his life.

This really bothered him and he
questioned the LORD about it:

"LORD, you said that once I decided to follow
you, you'd walk with me all the way.
But I have noticed that during the most
troublesome times in my life,
there is only one set of footprints.
I don't understand why when
I needed you most you would leave me."

The LORD replied:

"My son, my precious child,
I love you and I would never leave you.
During your times of trial and suffering,
when you see only one set of footprints,
it was then that I carried you."

About the Authors

Iqbal Atcha is a speaker, author, coach and entrepreneur. He has owned and operated several businesses specializing in healthcare, education and professional speaking. Iqbal is President of Converging Worlds, a company dedicated to helping people redefine the human connection through diversity and motivation. Iqbal is an active member of the National Speakers Association, Toastmasters International, and the American Pharmacists Association. Over the years, Iqbal has personally touched thousands of lives and positively impacted numerous organizations through his speaking engagements and one-on-one coaching sessions.

Amy K. Atcha is a legal guardian, life coach, speaker and author. She is the President and Founder of Customized Caring, Inc., a firm specializing in guardianship and power of attorney services, personal coaching and more. Amy is the author of the estate planning book entitled, *Me: Facts and Forecasts, A Guide for Now and Later.* Amy's passion is helping others succeed.

Visit Us:

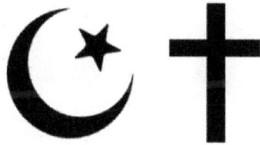

Converging Worlds, Inc.
www.convergingworlds.com

Customized Caring, Inc.
www.customizedcaring.com

www.ingramcontent.com/pod-product-compliance
Lightning Source LLC
Chambersburg PA
CBHW060936040426
42445CB00011B/889

* 9 7 8 0 6 1 5 6 1 3 1 5 4 *